A
CHRISTIAN FAMILY
IN BRITAIN

A CHRISTIAN FAMILY IN BRITAIN

Stephen W. Harrison
and
David Shepherd

RMEP

Religious and Moral Education Press
An Imprint of Pergamon Press

Religious and Moral Education Press
Hennock Road, Exeter EX2 8RP
An Imprint of Pergamon Press

Pergamon Press Ltd
Headington Hill Hall, Oxford OX3 0BW

Pergamon Press Inc.
Maxwell House, Fairview Park, Elmsford, New York 10523

Pergamon Press Canada Ltd
Suite 104, 150 Consumers Road, Willowdale, Ontario M2J 1P9

Pergamon Press (Australia) Pty Ltd
P.O. Box 544, Potts Point, N.S.W. 2011

Pergamon Press GmbH
Hammerweg 6, D-6242 Kronberg, Federal Republic of Germany

Copyright © 1986 Stephen W. Harrison and David Shepherd

First published 1986

Printed in Great Britain by A. Wheaton & Co. Ltd, Hennock Road, Exeter

ISBN 0 08-029297-6 non net
ISBN 0 08-029298-4 net

Contents

	PREFACE	1
1	EASTER CELEBRATIONS	3
2	EASTER TRADITIONS	11
3	EASTER MONDAY	17
4	GOING ABROAD	25
5	WHITSUNTIDE	31
6	CONFIRMATION	39
7	BELIEFS AND DOUBTS	48
8	ACTIVITY WEEK	54
9	SUNDAY	58
10	SCHOOL VISIT	64
11	DEATH OF A FRIEND	69
12	AN OLD CHURCH	73
13	MARRIAGE	85
14	CHRISTMAS	94
15	CHRISTIANITY IN BRITAIN	106
	RESOURCES/USEFUL ADDRESSES	113
	GLOSSARY	116

To Pat and Jennie

ACKNOWLEDGEMENTS

It would be impossible in a book of this nature to acknowledge all who have helped in its production. We would, however, like to mention the following:

The clergy at Emmanuel Shared Church, Weston Favell District Centre, Northampton, especially the Revd M. Glover (Church of England rector)
The Revd D. Black (Director of Department of Mission, Baptist Union)
The Revd B. George (Education Adviser, Baptist Union)
Father J. Cassidy (Milton Keynes)
Mr F. Desai (Community Relations Officer, Preston and West Lancashire)
Major J. B. Waldron and the Save the Children Fund (Camberwell, London)
Mr P. D. Wenham (Senior Adviser, Buckinghamshire County Council)
Mr I. Birnie (County Adviser in Religious Education, Lancashire County Council)
Mr M. Morrin (County Adviser, Cheshire County Council)
Mr P. E. Pawley (Headteacher, St Mary and St Giles Middle School, Milton Keynes)

But in the final analysis it is the authors who are responsible for any textual errors. All characters in this book are fictional. Words in bold type are included in the glossary (bold type is used the first time each word appears).

The extract from the New English Bible, Second Edition, Copyright © 1970, is reproduced by permission of Oxford and Cambridge University Presses.

Stephen W. Harrison is County Adviser, Lancashire County Council.

David Shepherd is Headteacher at Hanslope County Combined School, Milton Keynes, Buckinghamshire.

Photographs are reproduced by kind permission of the following:

Keith Ellis	Christian Aid
Sarah Thorley	Church Army
The Revd Nigel Mead	Coventry Cathedral
The Revd David Warner	*Lancashire Evening Post*
Julie and Christopher Bovey	The Mansell Collection
Richard Sadler	The National Gallery of Ireland
BBC Hulton Picture Library	P.J. Photography
Bodleian Library	The Salvation Army
The British Council of Churches	The Western Times Co. Ltd

Line drawings by Creative Marketing and Advertising

Preface

The need for a book on Christianity to complement those dealing with the world's other major faiths has been apparent for some time. In considering Islam, Buddhism, Judaism, Hinduism and Sikhism many authors have endeavoured to portray religious and cultural practices and at the same time to give some insight into what it means to be a member of a particular religion. This has been our aim in writing *A Christian Family in Britain*. Using an imaginary family we attempt to show what is is like to be a Christian in Britain – and, we trust, demonstrate why so many commit their lives to Christianity.

As with all faiths, this creates a problem: there is no such thing as a typical Christian family. What we have done, therefore, is to describe through narrative and dialogue events, thoughts and feelings which *could* be experienced by Christian families in Britain. We have chosen a "middle-of-the-road" family, but do not mean to imply that this is how all Christians in Britain act, merely how they might.

Our family (Mr and Mrs Thomas, Susan and Gary) are members of the Church of England. A number of their friends are not; for instance, Paul is a Baptist and Graham a Roman Catholic. By these as well as other means a number of the practices of various Christian denominations are described.

We are very conscious that Christianity in Britain exists within a multi-cultural and multi-racial society. Ignoring this in the text would have been a major omission. The reader will not be surprised to discover, therefore, that one of Susan's friends is Nina, a Hindu.

In this book we follow the Thomas family from Easter until Christmas, chronicling major events in that year. This approach allows us to relate the fundamental beliefs and customs of Christianity in a living and positive way. The book stresses action and also highlights some future challenges for Christians in Britain.

We envisage that *A Christian Family in Britain* will make a useful contribution to religious education and humanities courses, particularly within the 10–14 age-group. With this in mind we have included some "Suggestions for Further Study" at convenient points throughout the text. These suggestions, many of which are directed towards investigating Christianity within a multi-faith society, represent only a few of the potential avenues of inquiry; the issues raised by a book of this type are almost unlimited.

This book is intended to portray Christianity as a relevant and practical religion in Britain. Those who have experienced Christianity for themselves will readily identify with much of the text; we trust that it will be a valuable introduction for those who have not.

Stephen W. Harrison
David Shepherd

1
Easter Celebrations

"Wake up, Susan, it's five o'clock. Time to get up."

Mrs Thomas was already dressed. As she went past Gary's room she knocked on the door, but there was no reply. Gary found it difficult to get out of bed on a normal day, so she could hardly expect him to be wide awake at five in the morning!

On her way downstairs Mrs Thomas called Susan again, and added, "Susan, when you're dressed, will you wake Nina? Oh, and please give Gary another knock or he'll never be ready in time."

The Thomas family always get up very early on **Easter Day**. This year their routine was slightly different, because Susan's friend Nina was staying with them. It was to be Nina's first experience of Easter celebrations.

At last everyone was up and dressed.

"I don't know if it's the same at Hindu festivals, Nina," said Mrs Thomas, "but we don't usually have breakfast until after we've been to worship." She hoped Nina would share in the Easter celebrations as if she were one of the family, but she didn't want her to think that they always went without breakfast!

"That's OK, Mrs Thomas," answered Nina. "I'm not hungry yet anyway, and I'd like to do whatever Susan does at Easter. I'll try to learn all about what Easter means to Christians by doing what you do."

Mr Thomas had already been out to see what the weather was like. It was very cold but at least it was dry. Everyone had put on thick sweaters and good, strong shoes, Nina and

Susan had scarves wrapped round their necks and Gary was wearing a woolly hat.

Mr Thomas grinned and said to Nina, "There's a custom that special bonnets should be worn at Easter. I'm glad to see Gary is keeping up the tradition!"

By twenty past five they were all in the car. They drove out of town and along country lanes for about 16 kilometres. They parked in the large car-park at the foot of a steep hill and began the walk up to the summit. It was still quite dark and many of the people arriving for the Easter worship were carrying torches.

On the way up the hill the Thomases introduced Nina to several of their friends, and they helped her feel part of the celebrations. She noticed that everyone seemed happy. There was the same sense of joy and togetherness that she associated with Navaratri and Divali, her favourite Hindu festivals, and she asked Mrs Thomas whether the happy atmosphere was usual at Christian festivals.

"I suppose it is, Nina. People are especially happy on Easter Sunday, of course, because today is our most important day. It is the day that marks the real beginning for Christians and all we believe in."

As they neared the top of the hill they could hear singing. Ahead of them stood a crowd already more than four hundred strong and growing larger by the minute. They were grouped in a wide semicircle around a wooden table which had been carried up the hill the previous evening to act as an **altar.**

Mrs Thomas told Nina more about the meaning of Easter. "For Christians, the most important event that has ever happened took place on a Sunday long ago. We call it the **resurrection**, the 'rising up' or 'coming to life again', of Jesus Christ. We believe that Jesus was both the Son of God and a real man who lived on earth. His death and resurrection are seen as proof of God's love for everyone in the world. You see, Nina, we believe we can all receive the new life God gave Jesus when He raised him from the dead."

4

The Paschal (Easter) candle, lit in churches on the Saturday before Easter Day, symbolizes the light of the resurrection.

"Jesus was crucified, wasn't he?" asked Nina.

"Yes, that's right. Thousands of people throughout the Roman Empire were killed in this way. Most of them were slaves and criminals. **Crucifixion** was a very painful death. The victims were fastened to a wooden cross, either with ropes, or – as in Jesus's case – with rough nails driven through their hands and feet, and left to die."

"Jesus wasn't a slave or a criminal, was he?"

"No, but he wasn't popular with either the Jewish religious leaders or the civil – Roman – leaders of the day. In different ways Jesus seemed to pose a threat to both groups. The religious leaders were hostile towards him because he preached a different message to theirs, and the Romans distrusted anyone with a large number of followers in case they started a revolution.

"Jesus was arrested, tried by the Roman governor, Pontius Pilate, and condemned to death. He was crucified on **Good Friday**. Three days later he rose from the dead."

"How did Good Friday get its name? It sounds like anything but a good day to me."

"The word 'good' meant 'holy' in Old English," explained Mrs Thomas.

"I understand what you said about Jesus's resurrection, but I don't see why it affects Christians so much."

"Well, Christians believe that if Jesus, with God's help, rose from the dead to live again, with God's help they too will live again after death. The **Bible**, the holy book of Christianity, tells us that Christians will live again in heaven. ... We'd better stop chatting now, Nina, or we shall miss something."

Everyone faced the small wooden cross that stood in the centre of the table. In the East, dawn began to break. The rising of the sun was the signal to give thanks to God for the resurrection of Jesus and the promise of new life for all Christians.

Mr Thomas stepped forward and read this passage from the Bible:

When the Sabbath was over, Mary of Magdala, Mary the mother of James, and Salome bought aromatic oils intending to go and anoint him; and very early on the Sunday morning, just after sunrise, they came to the tomb. They were wondering among themselves who would roll away the stone for them from the entrance of the tomb, when they looked up and saw that the stone, huge as it was, had been rolled back already. They went into the tomb, where they saw a youth sitting on the right-hand side, wearing a white robe; and they were dumbfounded. But he said to them, "Fear nothing; you are looking for Jesus of Nazareth, who was crucified. He has risen; he is not here; look, there is the place where they laid him. But go and give this message to his disciples and Peter: 'He will go on before you into Galilee and you will see him there, as he told you.'" Then they went out and ran away from the tomb, beside themselves with terror. They said nothing to anybody, for they were afraid.

(Mark 16:3–8)

After the reading, the worshippers joined together in reciting the **Creed**, which is a statement of Christian beliefs. Nina didn't understand it all, but some of the ideas seemed clear to her:

"We believe in one God, the Father, the almighty, maker of heaven and earth... . We believe in one Lord, Jesus Christ, the only Son of God... by the power of the Holy Spirit he became incarnate of the Virgin Mary, and was made man. For our sake he was crucified under Pontius Pilate; he suffered death and was buried. On the third day he rose again in accordance with the Scriptures; he ascended into heaven and is seated at the right hand of the Father. ... We believe in the Holy Spirit, the Lord, the giver of life, who proceeds from the Father and the Son. ... We believe in one holy catholic and apostolic Church. ... We look for the resurrection of the dead, and the life of the world to come. Amen."

Like many Hindus, Nina believes in only one God, but she believes that God can appear in different forms. The statues she prays to in the temple represent different aspects of the same God. To her, the most important statue is the one of Lord Krishna.

Hindus believe that Krishna lived as a human being,

Spring flowers around a church font at Easter

8

experiencing all the joys and sorrows of life. Mischievous as a boy, he grew up into a handsome man and attracted all the girls of his village. Hindus pray to Krishna as a God who, because he lived on earth as a man, can understand human emotions. Nina could see that Christians might pray to Jesus in a similar way.

The service was led by Mr Rees, the **vicar**. Nina realized he was a vicar because he was wearing a clerical collar, or "dog-collar". Mr Rees's wife and children were also taking part in the early-morning worship.

Mr Rees placed a loaf of bread and a flagon of wine on the altar and blessed them. After a special prayer for Easter Day, thanking God for Jesus, he split the loaf in two, saying, "We break this bread to share in the body of Christ."

The congregation replied, "Though we are many, we are one body, because we all share in one bread."

Many of the worshippers stepped forward and the vicar gave each of them a small piece of bread and a sip of wine from a large silver cup, called a **chalice**. This reminded Nina of the food offered to the gods in Hindu temples, where the food is distributed among the worshippers after the service. Sharing food during worship brings people together.

When the last person had received bread and wine the vicar said a thanksgiving prayer. Then he blessed the congregation, and the service was over. Everyone drifted away in small groups, wishing one another a happy Easter, and went down the hillside to their cars. Nina and Susan helped a woman whose husband was in a wheelchair. When they had seen the couple safely into their car, they waved goodbye.

Twenty minutes later Nina and the Thomases were home again. Mr Thomas prepared a pot of coffee while Susan poured out bowls of cereal. They all enjoyed their breakfast: climbing the hill at that time of the morning had given them a real appetite.

Gary knew exactly what he was going to do next. "I feel as if I've been up all day, but look at the time – it's only eight o'clock! I'm going back to bed. Give me a call at half past eleven, will you, somebody? I'm playing football this afternoon and I need my rest."

Shortly afterwards Mr Thomas disappeared into the living-room to put his feet up with a book, but the others decided to have a second cup of coffee. Nina thought it might be a good time to ask a few questions about what she had seen on the hilltop that morning.

2
Easter Traditions

"Sometimes Hindu women and girls fast before a festival so that they can think more carefully about the meaning behind the celebrations," said Nina. "For instance, on Fridays in one month Mum and I eat only fruit, and I know that Muslims fast during Ramadan. They don't eat or drink during the hours of daylight. Do you fast before festivals like Easter?"

"Some Christians do, but we don't," replied Mrs Thomas. "It used to be quite common for Christians to fast during Lent, the period before Easter. Easter was considered to be a good time for the Church to receive new members. To prepare themselves, **candidates** would fast during Lent and receive instruction in Christianity. They were received into the Church on Holy Saturday, the day before Easter Sunday.

"As time went by, this period of self-denial was extended to all Church members as a means of preparing for Easter. The rules were quite strict: all meat, fish, eggs and dairy produce were forbidden. Gradually the rules were relaxed. For example, people were later allowed to eat fish during Lent."

"Had that anything to do with the custom of **Roman Catholics** eating fish on Fridays?" asked Susan.

"Yes, in a way. On fast-days Roman Catholics in particular remember Jesus's death. Because meat reminded them of the body of Jesus they traditionally ate some other food, such as fish, on fast-days. Jesus died on Good Friday, so Friday became the day when Roman Catholics ate fish.

"When I was a young girl, my family never ate meat during Lent. Children were expected to choose a favourite

11

food, like ice cream, cake or sweets, and promise to give it up for the whole of Lent. We didn't fast as strictly as people did in the Middle Ages, but we did make a sacrifice that helped us prepare our minds for Easter. Every time I refused a cake or an ice cream it made me think about Jesus and how he prepared for his death."

"As I see it," said Nina, "when they fasted, Christians didn't go without food altogether, they just cut back."

"Yes, that's right," agreed Mrs Thomas. "Christians' attitude to Lent has changed over the years, though. Today we see Lent as a time to do something positive, to help others, rather than simply giving up something. In this family we make a special donation to charity every Wednesday in Lent. Giving the money is our sacrifice, and it helps someone in need."

"I think I understand about fasting now," said Nina, "but could you tell me a little more about Lent?"

Mrs Thomas began by explaining the origin of the name. "'Lent' comes from a word meaning 'to lengthen'. It was once a name for spring, the time of year when the days start to lengthen.

"Lent lasts for forty days (not including Sundays), beginning on Ash Wednesday and ending on Holy Saturday. It recalls the forty days and nights during which, according to the Bible, Jesus went without food and drink in order to prepare for his ministry.

"Lent always occurs in the early part of the year. The date of Easter Day is determined by the phases of the moon. In the fourth century it was decided that Easter should always be the Sunday following the first full moon after 21 March."

"They probably chose that date because it's the first day of spring," remarked Susan. "Now let me work this out. If a full moon shines on 21 March and that day is also a Saturday, Easter Sunday will be 22 March."

"Well done," smiled Mrs Thomas. "The earliest possible date for Easter is 22 March. The last possible date is 25 April.

12

"The preparations for Easter traditionally began on Pancake Day, **Shrove Tuesday**, to use its correct title. In many parts of the Christian world Shrove Tuesday was the last day people were allowed to eat meat. That's how we get the word 'carnival': it comes from '*carne levare*', which is Latin for 'put away meat'. You've probably heard of the famous Mardi Gras carnivals they have in New Orleans and Rio de Janeiro, for example. Mardi Gras is another name for Shrove Tuesday. It means 'Fat Tuesday'."

Nina looked puzzled. "How can a day be fat?"

"The day isn't fat, silly," laughed Susan. "It means that everyone had to use up all their butter and animal fat on that day, before the fasting began on Ash Wednesday. Colin Phillips was telling me about Mardi Gras in Trinidad the other day. That's where he comes from. He told me that more than a hundred thousand people join in the carnival, dressed in fantastic costumes. Some of the costumes take months to make."

Pancake race on Shrove Tuesday

Nina was wondering what "Shrove" meant. Mrs Thomas explained that it came from the old word to "shrive".

"In Britain Shrove Tuesday was the day when people went to church to be shriven. This meant confessing their sins to the **priest**, who would absolve them and give them a penance, or task to do as a punishment. After church everyone used to play games, run races and eat up all the food they weren't allowed to eat in Lent. They mixed flour, eggs and milk into a batter and made pancakes. Nowadays we still enjoy pancakes on Shrove Tuesday, even though most of us don't fast during Lent. The celebrations ended at midnight on Shrove Tuesday and the serious preparations for Easter began on **Ash Wednesday.**

"That's another name I should explain. It comes from the old custom of showing grief or mourning by wearing sackcloth and rubbing your head with ashes. Later on, people who had committed serious sins were marked with a cross in ash on the forehead on Ash Wednesday and the priest would give them a hard penance to do. Some Christian churches continue the tradition today. We know some Roman Catholics who always go to church on Ash Wednesday. During the service the priest dips his thumb in a mixture of ashes and holy water and makes a small mark on each worshipper's forehead."

"Mothering Sunday is an important day in Lent, isn't it, Mum?"

"Yes, it's a special day for all Christian mothers," Mrs Thomas told Nina. "Susan, Gary and Mr Thomas always give me cards and presents as well as doing the cooking and washing-up. Christians used to visit their 'mother' church – the one they attended as children – on Mothering Sunday. I suppose the idea of honouring human mothers developed from that.

"Mothering Sunday is also called Mid-Lent, Refreshment or Simnel Sunday, because it occurs about half-way through Lent, on the fourth Sunday of Lent, and is often marked by eating some rich food, such as simnel cake."

"Simnel cake is lovely," Susan told her friend. "It's a rich fruit cake with a layer of marzipan and some decorations on top."

"Mothering Sunday isn't quite the same as Mother's Day," continued Mrs Thomas. "Mother's Day began in America, where it is held on the second Sunday in May. It is a day devoted to human mothers and doesn't have any particular religious significance."

"Are there extra church services during Lent?" asked Nina.

During the Mothering Sunday service at their Methodist church, these children were given posies to present to their mothers.

"There are the normal Sunday services, of course. On Mothering Sunday we try to visit my parents and attend my 'mother' church, although this has not always been possible, especially when Susan and Gary were younger. Mr Thomas and I go to special Lenten services at church. They are held on Wednesday evenings at half past six. Gary and Susan don't come because of their homework, although some young people do attend."

"It's the same at my temple," said Nina. "We have special months when a lot of people go to worship during the week. Even so, Sunday is still the busiest day at the temple. Are the Easter celebrations over now?"

"No, not quite. The festival goes on until tomorrow," replied Mrs Thomas. "You'll enjoy Easter Monday, Nina. We do something rather special."

3
Easter Monday

Easter Monday is celebrated very differently from Easter Sunday. Everyone slept in, including Gary. They had breakfast at half past nine and afterwards, while Gary and Nina helped Mrs Thomas clear the table, Susan and Mr Thomas packed the picnic box and loaded the car for their day out.

"I've known the name 'Easter' since I was a baby, but, to be honest, no one has ever told me what it means," admitted Nina.

"I'm not surprised," said Mrs Thomas. "Many Christians don't know the origin of the word either. I'll try to explain. Christianity took a long time to be accepted in some parts of Europe. The people who lived in northern Europe already had their own religions. The Christian Church found it easier to persuade people to worship in the Christian way if aspects of the old religions and their festivals were allowed to continue.

"The arrival of spring used to be celebrated with a festival at which a goddess called Eostre or Eastre was worshipped. Around the eighth century A.D. this spring festival became the time to remember the death and resurrection of Jesus, but the ancient name was still used. That's why here in Britain we call it Easter."

"My dad once told me that in Roman Catholic churches in India there are statues of Mary that look just like our Hindu goddesses," said Nina. "Do you think that's the same sort of thing?"

17

"I suppose it is. People are happier to accept a new religion if there is something familiar about it."

Just then Mr Thomas came in from the garage to round them all up. "Right, everyone, the picnic box and the Easter eggs are in the car. Let's be on our way."

They drove to the far side of town, where they parked the car and walked along the river-bank. There were hundreds of people picnicking on the grass in the park.

Nina wondered why this park was so popular. "The one near my house is nice and flat. It's very steep here. Our picnic will probably roll away!"

"That's the reason for coming here," grinned Susan. "These hills are perfect for rolling our eggs."

Susan spread a blanket on the grass and Mr Thomas produced the bag of hard-boiled eggs. Susan and Nina had spent an hour dyeing and painting the eggs on Saturday. Nina hadn't been told why, but she'd enjoyed doing it.

Other friends and relations, including the children's grandfather, began to arrive and by half past eleven there were twenty-six adults and children in their picnic group.

Grandad Thomas was given the job of judging the eggs. He didn't know who had decorated which egg, so his decision was fair. He chose a blue and yellow egg painted by Susan's young cousin Martin. The prize was an enormous chocolate Easter egg.

Another prize was given to the child whose egg rolled furthest down the hill. Nine-year-old Emma won that one.

"Don't worry, Nina," Susan consoled her, "we've still got a chance of winning an Easter egg. The next game is smashing – literally!"

All the young people faced each other in pairs and rolled their eggs together until one cracked. When an egg cracked its owner dropped out of the contest.

After half an hour Nina and Gary were the only ones left. Gary was confident of winning. He'd been the winner for the last two years. The eggs rolled, collided, a crack appeared – in Gary's egg! Nina had won. She was delighted.

Families gather for picnics and egg-rolling on Easter Monday.

"I don't know what my mum would think," said Nina, sitting down with her prize beside Mrs Thomas. "She's a very strict vegetarian. She won't even cook an egg, let alone eat one. What do all these eggs, boiled eggs, chocolate eggs, have to do with Easter?"

"There are two reasons, I think," replied Mrs Thomas. "The first takes us back to the idea of a new life in Jesus. In the days before electricity and battery farming spring was always the time for new life to appear. The eggs hatched in spring and the newly born chicks were a sign of new life.

"The other reason takes us back to the events at Jesus's tomb. Do you remember Mr Thomas reading from the Bible about the women who visited the tomb? When they arrived there the tomb was open. This was a real shock, because the entrance had been sealed with a large stone. When we roll our Easter eggs we recall the rolling away of that stone and the new life of Jesus."

"Do you know what happened at the first Easter?" Grandad Thomas asked Nina.

19

"I do know something about it, because a great deal of the R.E. taught in my school is about **Christianity**. I can't really understand what happened, though."

While Nina ate her chocolate, Grandad Thomas told her about the events leading up to Jesus's death.

Jesus was in his early thirties. He had been preaching for a couple of years and many of the ideas he taught were regarded with suspicion by the Jewish religious leaders. For instance, the Bible tells us that on one Sabbath day Jesus healed a man who had been crippled for years. He then asked him to take up his bed and walk. This offended the Jewish religious leaders, who regarded any form of work on the Sabbath (their holy day, Saturday) as completely wrong. They regarded Jesus's healing as work.

Jesus spent the last week of his life in Jerusalem, which was the Jewish religious centre of the time. According to the Bible, he rode into the city on a donkey. The people gave Jesus a great welcome, spreading palm branches on the ground for him to ride over.

Christians remember this event on the Sunday before Easter, which is called **Palm Sunday**. On this day in many churches crosses made from palm-leaf fronds are given to the congregation. Palm Sunday marks the beginning of **Holy Week**. During this week Christians try to think very deeply about the events leading up to Jesus's death.

On the Thursday of Holy Week Jesus ate a meal with his twelve most devoted followers, who are known as the **Twelve Disciples** or the **Apostles**. Christians call this meal the **Last Supper**. Jesus gave his disciples bread and told them, "This is my body". Then he gave them wine, saying, "This is my blood." Ever since then Christians meeting together have shared bread and wine and have remembered Jesus's words.

The bread and wine can be seen as symbols of Jesus's approaching death. Some Christians believe Jesus knew he was destined to die, that his life would have to be sacrificed in order to give the world the chance of new life.

Listening to Grandad Thomas describe the Last Supper,

Nina understood why bread and wine had been shared on the hilltop during the Easter Sunday service. "That reminded me of what we do at the Hindu temple during our *puja*, our worship," she said thoughtfully. "We offer fruit, vegetables and sweets to our gods and then all the worshippers share and eat the food. I visited a Sikh gurdwara once. During the ceremony, everyone was given a sweet food called *karah parshad*, and afterwards they had a meal together in the dining-room."

"I suppose that for many religious groups eating together is a sign of sharing in the religion," replied Grandad Thomas. "We Christians share the bread and wine as members of a family, the family of Jesus. Meals are an important and enjoyable part of family life for most people, and as Christians we are all brothers and sisters." He told Nina about a significant incident that took place just before the Last Supper.

Before they ate the meal, Jesus washed his disciples' feet. He told them that they should do the same to others to show that, as his followers, they really cared about other people. Because of this instruction, Christians have always called the Thursday of Holy Week **Maundy Thursday**, which means "Commandment Thursday".

Since the time of Jesus, Maundy Thursday has been commemorated by Christians all over the world. Priests, kings and monks used to wash the feet of twelve poor people on this day, and it is also a traditional occasion to give money to the poor. In Britain today the Queen gives special Maundy money to twelve elderly people. Each of them receives a small leather purse containing specially minted coins to the value of one penny for each year of the Queen's age, and another purse containing five pounds in ordinary money.

During the meal, Jesus told his disciples that he knew one of them was going to betray him. One of the disciples, Judas, had made a deal with the chief priests in Jerusalem, agreeing to lead them to Jesus in return for a reward.

21

H.M. the Queen and the Dean of Exeter Cathedral after a Maundy service

Maundy money

Late that night, after the Last Supper, Jesus was arrested. He was taken to the home of the high priest and charged with saying things that were against Jewish religious law. The high priest, Caiaphas, had Jesus put in chains and handed him over to the Romans.

It was because Jesus was crucified that the cross became the most important symbol of Christianity. All religions have special symbols. Hindus have the sacred word "*Om*", the Jews have the Star of David, Muslims the crescent moon and star, and so on.

Although Jesus died on the cross, Christians do not regard it as a depressing symbol. To them, it symbolizes not death itself but Jesus's victory over death. They believe that when Jesus lived on earth the world was an evil place. People had turned away from God; they were sinful and deserved to be punished. Jesus took on that punishment, suffering on their behalf. He died so that the world could have another chance.

What happened after Jesus's death gave people new hope for the future. His death was not final. Christians believe he rose from the dead three days after the Crucifixion. The custom of rolling eggs on Easter Monday is a celebration of his resurrection, his living again. Christianity teaches that, just as Jesus lived on after his earthly life, so shall we live on after our death. That is why the cross is not a sad symbol but a symbol of hope.

SUGGESTIONS FOR FURTHER STUDY

1 The Thomas family celebrated Easter in a rather unusual way. Find out how other Christian denominations observe this festival and write an account of the customs surrounding the Easter period.

2 Some Christians celebrate Easter at different times from the Roman Catholic Church and the Anglican Church. Use an encyclopaedia to find out how and when members of the Orthodox Church celebrate Easter.

3 Choose three of the world's religions and write about the part fasting plays in each: when and why it is observed and what it involves.

4 Draw the religious symbols of Christianity, Islam, Judaism, Hinduism, Sikhism and Buddhism. What is the significance of each symbol?

5 Some countries have religious symbols on their national flags. Identify as many flags as you can that display such symbols.

4
Going Abroad

Gary spent hours shut up in his room on the Friday after Easter. In the evening Mrs Thomas decided to make sure he was all right. When she opened his bedroom door she was surprised to see the floor covered with newspapers and large sheets of white paper spread out on top. There were pots of paint lined up on the window-ledge.

"What on earth are you doing?" she asked.

"I didn't want you to know about this, Mum."

"I'm not surprised. Fancy painting on your bedroom floor. If you've ruined the carpet I'll...."

"No, I didn't mean that I didn't want you to know I've been painting, I meant I didn't want you to know about my plan until I've finished. Please trust me, Mum. Give me one more hour."

An hour later Gary walked into the lounge carrying three big posters. Each one, written in large colourful letters, read, "Secondhand book and toy sale. In aid of a good cause. Gary Thomas's garage, 2 p.m., Saturday."

"What's the good cause?" asked Mr Thomas suspiciously. "It wouldn't be new games for your micro, would it?"

"No, Dad, I'm surprised you could think such a thing," protested Gary. "As a matter of fact, it's to help send Peter Kennedy to Africa. Everyone at church has been raising money for him and I'd like to do my share. I decided yesterday to sell my old books and toys. I'm going to charge fair prices. Everyone in my class knows about the sale, and these posters will let everyone who lives around here know as well. All the money I raise will go to Peter."

The sale was very successful. Gary was pleased with himself. It had been his idea and he had carried it through alone. The money he would give to Peter was his own personal contribution.

One Wednesday evening a fortnight later, the Thomas family joined many friends from their church at Peter Kennedy's house.

Peter was well known in the area. He had been to the same school as Susan and later studied engineering at university. After his graduation he had a long talk with Mr Rees, the vicar of St Martin's Church.

Peter explained to Mr Rees that he'd been thinking about Jesus's instruction to love your neighbour. While he enjoyed raising money for St Martin's, looking after the grounds, helping in the youth club and so on, he had the feeling that his skills and enthusiasm might be more useful elsewhere.

Mr Rees agreed with him and suggested that there might well be communities in some parts of the world who desperately need the skills of a trained engineer. He contacted the local development education officer to find out if Peter could be useful in some way.

Soon a letter arrived at Peter's house giving him details of a village in Africa which was in great need of a clean-water supply. Peter said he would like to go and help, and Mr Rees asked the members of the church to raise money towards fuel and equipment for the project. In this way Peter would become a link between the members of St Martin's Church and another community thousands of kilometres away who needed their help.

The party had been under way for over an hour before Susan managed to have a private word with Peter. She wasn't as enthusiastic about the project as Gary was. There were some questions she wanted to ask.

"Peter, aren't you going to lose a lot of money by living abroad for two years?" she began. "If you stayed in this country you could get a really good job and you'd soon have a nice house and a new car."

26

Villagers in a drought-stricken region of West Africa construct a barrage to contain seasonal water for irrigation. They are helped by funds and expert assistance from Christian Aid.

"A lot of my friends have asked me the same question, Susan," replied Peter. "I was tempted to start work straight away, and with my qualifications I could soon find a well-paid job, despite all the unemployment. I've had a long, hard think about it and I've decided that making a comfortable life for myself isn't enough.

"I realize how privileged I am. I was lucky to be born fit and healthy in a rich country. I've been taught skills which are very rare in some parts of the world. To me, loving my neighbour means more than just loving the people who attend my church. It means working alongside the people who need me most."

"Yes, but somebody told me that in the village you're going to the people are not even Christians. Is that true?"

"Quite true. I'm sure Jesus would not have wanted his followers to mix only with their own kind. Remember, he chose to eat with the poor and the kinds of people whom no one else respected. I want to help people, not just Christians, but anyone who needs me, whatever their race or religion."

"I suppose you'll try to convert them to Christianity, won't you?" Susan asked.

"Now, that is a question! Let me tell you what I plan to do, though of course when I get there who knows what will happen. I shall do my best to work with the local people to construct a clean-water supply to the village. If they ask me why I'm doing it, I'll tell them it's because of the teachings of Jesus and what those teachings mean to me. If anyone wants to know more about my beliefs I shall explain, but if they don't ask, I shall be satisfied simply to help. I'm not going there to do a deal like some **missionaries** did in the past – you know, 'Become a Christian and I'll give you food and clothing'. The work I do will be my way of worshipping God and if others want to know about my God then of course I'll explain."

"Some of my friends say we shouldn't help people in other countries, we've got enough problems here in Britain," said Susan. "Sometimes I think they're right."

28

British Guides collect money for Christian Aid.

"I know many people think like that, but I don't share their point of view. We certainly do have problems in this country: high unemployment, bad housing in many large towns, and so on. I know the average standard of living in Britain is lower than in most other Western European countries. Even so, ours is a rich country. We can make life better for the poor if we choose to. I am going to help people who work hard every day but who have no electricity or running water and cannot be sure of having enough food to feed their families.

"I'm not going for ever, Susan. I shall be away for two years and I'll probably spend another thirty-five years working in Britain, earning a good wage, buying a house and a car, having all the things you mentioned earlier."

Susan seemed convinced. "Now you put it that way it seems to make more sense. I have a feeling that you will probably enjoy your two years abroad more than you would two years working here. I wouldn't be a bit surprised if you took on another project when your first one is finished."

"You may be right, Susan. You see, that's what being a Christian means to me."

5
Whitsuntide

Peter was due to fly out from Heathrow in mid-June, so **Whitsun** was the last Christian festival he would celebrate before his departure. The Thomases invited him and his family to join them for an evening meal on Whit Sunday.

Grandad Thomas gave everyone a glass of sherry before they sat down to eat. "I want to propose a toast to Peter, our guest of honour, as he will be leaving us soon. He takes with him our best wishes. As it is Whitsuntide, it is very appropriate that today we ask the **Holy Spirit** to guide, protect and help him."

Everyone raised their glasses and drank a toast to Peter.

The guests settled down to talk and Gary went to help his parents with the final preparations in the kitchen.

He was a bit confused by his grandfather's speech, and asked, "Mum, what did Grandad mean about Whitsuntide, and Peter being protected by the Holy Spirit?"

"What a question when I'm cooking a meal! I'll try to explain. At Easter we celebrated the resurrection of Jesus, didn't we? Well, according to the Bible, Jesus visited a lot of people after his resurrection. He stayed on earth for another forty days and then he went up to heaven. Christians remember that event on **Ascension Day**, which was the Thursday before last.

"Before he left his followers, Jesus told them not to worry. A comforter, or counsellor, was coming to support them. Because they didn't understand what Jesus was saying, his followers were rather confused. They were frightened, too. Many of them were expecting the Romans to arrest them and

31

perhaps crucify them as well, so they kept away from public places and met secretly to pray. Ten days after the ascension of Jesus, they celebrated the feast of **Pentecost**.

"This Jewish festival is still celebrated today. It recalls the

The Ascension. " ... as they watched, he was lifted up, and a cloud removed him from their sight" (Acts 1:9).

32

time when Moses received the Ten Commandments on Mount Sinai. Don't forget, Gary, that Jesus and all his early followers were Jews. They went to **synagogues** and to the **Temple** like other Jews. On occasions Jesus was even called a **rabbi**, the name for a Jewish teacher. From childhood, they would all have taken part in Jewish religious festivals and they naturally continued to celebrate them after his death.

"At Pentecost, something incredible happened to Jesus's followers. It's hard to say exactly what. The Bible says they were all filled with the Holy Spirit. Whatever happened, it gave them great confidence. They were no longer afraid to go out. In fact, they immediately started teaching about Jesus and what he meant to them. The small group of followers grew rapidly.

"That day was the first Whit Sunday. It marked the real beginning of the Christian Church, and is sometimes called the Church's birthday."

"The Holy Ghost is the same as the Holy Spirit, isn't it?"

"Yes, it's a force from God, and the third part of what Christians call the **Holy Trinity**. We believe that God's power and presence can be felt in three distinct ways, or as three persons: Father, Son and Holy Spirit. That's what we mean when we end a prayer by saying, 'In the name of the Father, the Son and the Holy Ghost'. God the Father sent his Son, Jesus, to live on earth as a human being, and the Holy Ghost is the symbol of God's power.

"Sometimes Christians explain the Trinity in historical terms: the power that guided the world before Jesus came to earth is the Father; Jesus is God during his lifetime on earth – the same power – and the Holy Spirit is the same power again, but God after Jesus's death on the cross."

"So Grandad asked the Holy Spirit to guide Peter Kennedy because that's how he sees God's power nowadays, and this is a particularly good time to ask for the Holy Spirit's help because it was at Whitsun that Jesus's followers first received the power of the Holy Spirit."

"You've got the idea," said Mrs Thomas, handing Gary a

33

Pentecost. The dove represents the Holy Spirit.

serving-dish. "Now, carry these roast potatoes to the table or they'll be stone cold by the time we sit down to eat!"

During the meal Gary asked his grandfather to tell him what Whitsuntide had been like in the past.

"When I was a boy Whit was a special occasion," Grandad Thomas began. "These days we have a Spring Bank Holiday at the end of May, but we always used to have a national holiday on the Monday after Whit Sunday, Whit Monday.

"In the Middle Ages, people who had decided to become Christians often joined the Church at Whitsun. Because they wore white for the ceremony, the day became known as 'White Sunday'. The two words later ran together into one, 'Whitsun'.

"To celebrate the birthday of the Church, Christians would give money towards the maintenance of church buildings. At many churches the churchwardens used to brew ale and sell it in the church grounds. All the money they made from this Whitsun Ale went to the church."

"Did children drink it?" Susan asked.

"Oh, yes. Until about the eighteenth century, when tea and coffee were introduced into Britain, ale was a traditional drink for all ages."

Gary nudged Susan. "That's why they call them the good old days."

"There would be Morris dancing and actors performing **miracle** or **mystery plays**," their grandfather continued.

"Was a mystery play like an old-fashioned spy film?"

"No, Gary, not at all. A mystery play acted out scenes from the Bible and helped ordinary people understand the religious meaning. Not a bit like James Bond, I'm afraid. We still have these plays in some towns today, in York, Chester and Wakefield, for example.

"In some parts of the country there are processions at Whitsuntide. All the members of a church walk around their district carrying banners or a cross, usually accompanied by a band and the church choir."

Jesus before Pontius Pilate and Caiaphas. A scene from a mystery play staged in the ruins of the old Coventry Cathedral.

Well-dressing at Tissington, Derbyshire, at the turn of the century. Psalms are read and a hymn is sung at each well in the village.

"Some Easter celebrations aren't entirely Christian. Is it the same with Whitsun?" asked Susan.

"All the customs I've mentioned so far come from our Christian past, but there is a pagan element to Whitsuntide, Susan. I lived in Derbyshire for a while and there they have an ancient custom called well-dressing. At Whitsun or Ascension they decorate wells with collages made entirely from natural materials, such as flowers, fir-cones and moss. The collages show scenes from the Bible. Long ago they would have shown scenes from the ancient religion of the area. Remember, people had religious beliefs before Christianity came to Britain. Many prayed to tree or water spirits. Others believed in the powers of the Norse gods, such as Thor and Freya, who were worshipped throughout Northern Europe.

"They chose to decorate wells because wells played an important part in their lives. Wells gave them water, which in turn gave them life. It used to be common for people to pray near wells and other water-sources."

"Water seems to play a special part in most religions," commented Susan. "Christians use it in baptism, Muslims drink from the Zamzam well in Mecca, Hindus bathe in the River Ganges and Buddhists celebrate the New Year with a water festival."

"Quite right, too," said Peter, who had been following the conversation with interest. "All this brings us back to why I'm leaving next week: to provide clean running water for people who as yet don't have any. Just imagine, water to drink, water for washing, water for the crops! With luck and the help of the Holy Spirit those people's lives will be transformed when I've completed my work."

Mr Thomas went over to the sideboard. "That's enough talk about water. I'm going to open a bottle of wine," he announced. "It may be the last Peter will taste for two years, so let's make this a meal to remember. Eat up, everyone, there's plenty more in the kitchen."

SUGGESTIONS FOR FURTHER STUDY

1 Peter Kennedy expressed his Christian beliefs in the way he chose to help others. Choose three people, someone from the past, someone alive today and someone you know personally, and describe how each has helped others. You can of course choose people who are not Christians.

2 The first person to take the message of Jesus to non-Jews was St Paul. He spent much of his life travelling and spreading the story of Jesus and his teachings. Find out where St Paul went on his journeys and locate the places on a modern map. Use the Acts of the Apostles in the New Testament to start you off.

3 If someone knocked on your door and told you he had brought the good news about a new religion, would you listen or send him away? Many people would refuse to listen, but if no one had listened to St Paul and other missionaries there would be no Christians in Britain today. Discuss this issue with members of your class.

4 Some religions, such as Christianity and Islam, are evangelistic religions: they try to persuade others to join them. Others, like Hinduism and Judaism, do not. Talk to followers of these religions and try to discover why they are/are not evangelistic.

5 Christianity appealed to poor people first and to the better-off later. Why do you think new religions and denominations tend to be more attractive to the poor?

6 Water holds a special place in religion. Choose three religions and describe how each uses water in its ceremonies.

6
Confirmation

"I hope these classes will be of help to you in your Christian lives. If they are, I shall consider them to have been successful. Goodbye for now, I'll see you all on Sunday." The vicar closed the door as Gary and the others left.

Gary had been attending Mr Rees's **confirmation** classes every Friday evening for the past two months. He had noticed that the subjects Mr Rees discussed most often were prayer, reading the Bible, the importance of going to church regularly, and helping others. These four, the vicar believes, are the most practical and the most important aspects of a Christian's life.

Six of Gary's friends had started going to the classes at the same time as him, but two dropped out after a few lessons because they couldn't attend every week. Mr Rees had stressed at the beginning that he expected everyone to come to most of the classes as they were all important.

Mr Rees normally holds two series of confirmation classes for young people each year. Most of the children are in the twelve-to-fifteen age-group, but occasionally one or two are a little younger, about nine years of age. He also gives one series of classes for adults each year. It is traditional for confirmation to take place at Easter, or at Whit, so Mr Rees usually tries to finish the adult class and one of the young people's classes just before Easter. This isn't always possible, of course, and Gary and his friends were to be confirmed on the second Sunday after Whitsun.

It was 7.30 when Gary arrived home from the vicarage. His friend Paul had called to see if he wanted to listen to some records.

"Hi, Gary. Your mum's been telling me that you're to be confirmed on Sunday."

"Yes, I'm a bit nervous."

Mrs Thomas pointed out that it was Gary who had decided he wanted to be confirmed and to attend all the preparation lessons. When he was **baptized**, on the other hand, he was very young and his parents had made the decision on his behalf.

Paul told Gary and Mrs Thomas that he would not be confirmed. "I'm a **Baptist** and we don't have confirmation in our Church, although we have something like it. We call it Church membership. When a person is old enough to decide they want to know more about being a Christian the minister explains what is involved. Before we are accepted as members we have to be baptized. I was baptized a few months ago."

They compared the ways in which Gary and Paul had been baptized – Gary by having the sign of the cross traced across his forehead in holy water from the **font** and Paul by total immersion in a baptismal tank.

"I don't suppose it matters what ceremonies different Churches use," Gary remarked. "What matters is the meaning behind the customs."

"That's very true," answered Mrs Thomas. "So far we have talked about the different practices of only two **denominations**, or Churches. There are many other variations: the practice of the Roman Catholic Church is similar to that of the **Church of England**, whereas the **Pentecostal Church** would regard all regular church attenders who acknowledge and accept the Church's fundamental beliefs as members. In other words, Pentecostals don't have to go to special lessons. Whether or not there is a ceremony, and however it is performed, confirmation or Church membership is a sign that the believer wants to become more closely involved in the Christian way of life."

Because Paul seemed to be interested in the Anglican

40

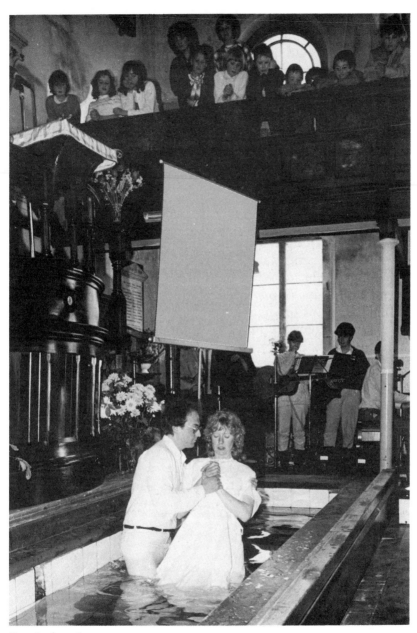

Baptist baptism ceremony

confirmation ceremony, Mrs Thomas suggested that he come and see Gary being confirmed. A number of Gary's friends and relations had promised to come and some of them attended other churches, or no church at all, so she didn't think Paul would feel out of place.

Paul looked at Gary to see how he would react to his mother's invitation. Gary nodded, encouraging him to accept.

"Well, if Gary really doesn't mind, I'd like to come," said Paul. "I've never been to a confirmation service before."

"Come on, Gary, wake up. It's eight o'clock," said Mr Thomas. "Your grandad will be here soon."

Sunday morning had come round quickly. Remembering that this was his big day, Gary was soon washed and dressed.

The doorbell rang while he was eating his breakfast. It was his grandparents. Soon other relations and friends, including Paul, arrived. At ten past ten they all drove to the church.

"Did your parents mind you coming along with us this morning?" asked Gary.

"No," replied Paul, "they were pleased you were being confirmed and thought it right that I should come and watch. They send you their best wishes for today."

"Soon the Thomases' convoy of cars arrived at the church. Gary was still a little nervous as he met the friends with whom he had attended confirmation classes. The four of them sat together on the front **pew**. Their families and friends sat with the rest of the congregation.

"How long will the service last?" whispered Paul to Mrs Thomas.

"Just over an hour, I should think," was the reply. "The confirmation will be followed by **Holy Communion**. The **bishop** is going to lead the service."

"I've never seen a bishop before."

"Only a bishop can confirm Church members. He is in charge of a **diocese**, which is made up of a number of **parishes**."

As the bishop and the vicar entered the church, the organist began to play the first hymn. The service was about to start.

After the first hymn the bishop began, "The Lord be with you."

Although he was still excited, Gary was feeling less nervous now. The service seemed to be passing quickly. The bishop gave a short **sermon** reminding the candidates for confirmation about their responsibilities as Christians. He referred to some of the things Mr Rees had taught them about prayer, Bible-reading, church attendance and helping others. He also reminded the candidates' parents to encourage their children to live Christian lives.

After this address came the part of the service Gary and his friends had planned during their classes. They had chosen a favourite hymn, prayer and Bible-reading. Mr Thomas read the passage from the Bible. Then the bishop turned to the candidates.

"You have come here to be confirmed," he began. "You must now declare before God and His Church that you accept the Christian faith into which you were baptized, and in which you will live and grow."

He asked Gary and each of his friends three questions about their Christian beliefs. After the replies he laid his hands on the head of each candidate.

It was Gary's turn. "Confirm, O Lord, your servant Gary with your Holy Spirit."

For Gary the rest of the service went by in a whirl. He was delighted to be a full member of the Church at last. He had attended church for a long time but he had never experienced anything like this before. He realized that he would not always live up to being the kind of Christian Mr Rees had spoken about in his confirmation classes but at least he would try his best.

It was lunch-time when the Thomas family and their friends arrived home.

Paul told Gary he had enjoyed the service. "How do you

Confirmation

feel?" he asked. "When I was baptized and became a member of my Church I felt pretty grown-up, because I'd made the decision myself."

"Yes, I feel the same," replied Gary. "Could I come to one of your services some time, perhaps a baptism service?"

"Sure. I'll let you know when the next one is being held."

44

Grandad Thomas was very pleased that his grandson had decided to become a full member of the Church. To mark the occasion he had bought Gary an expensive leather-bound Bible.

Gary thanked him and carefully put the Bible in the bookcase.

His grandfather promptly took it off the shelf.

"Oh no you don't, young man. That's only half my gift."

"What do you mean, Grandad?"

"You remember when you were given your first bike, don't you? Well, what did you need to do before you could go out on it?"

"Learn how to ride it, I suppose."

"Right. Well, that Bible I've just given you isn't like other books. You don't simply start at the beginning and read to the end like you do with a story-book. You need to know how to use it if you are going to gain anything from it."

"And I suppose you're going to show me, eh, Grandad?"

"Absolutely right, Gary. The first thing to realize is that although we call the Bible a book it is actually a collection of books written by a number of people at different times. That makes it different to the holy books of some other religions. The Qur'an of the Muslims, for example, is regarded as the actual word of God as spoken to one man, the Prophet Muhammad.

"If you look at your Bible you will see that it is divided into two major sections. The first is much larger than the second.

"The first section is called the **Old Testament**. It was completed before the birth of Jesus and contains thirty-nine books. The books of the Old Testament were written by Hebrew writers. These writings, along with others, are read by Jews today, so you can see that Christians still share some of their holy writings with Jews.

"Jews call the first five books of the Old Testament the Sefer Torah, or the Pentateuch. These books are thought to have been dictated by God to Moses on Mount Sinai.

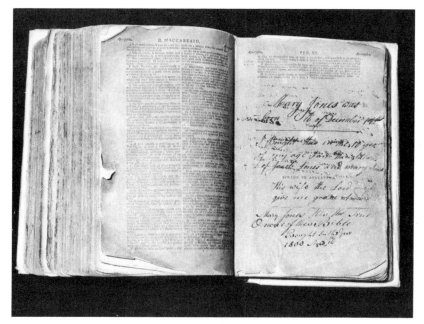

The Bible has been translated into many languages, including Welsh. In 1800 a Welsh girl called Mary Jones walked over 80 kilometres to buy this Bible with her hard-earned savings.

Another section of books is known as the Prophets. These contain the teachings of Hebrews who were regarded as inspired teachers capable of interpreting God's will. The prophets warned the Jewish people of what might happen if they failed to follow God's laws.

"The idea that runs right through the Old Testament is that God made a covenant, a sort of deal, or contract, with the Jewish people. He promised that if they remained faithful to Him they would become a great nation.

"The second part of the Christian Bible is quite short. It is called the **New Testament**, and contains twenty-seven books. Four of these, the **Gospels**, are about the life and teachings of Jesus. Another book, the Acts, tells how the early Church was formed and describes the events following the death of Jesus. Then there are twenty-one Epistles or letters, written by early Christian teachers to various Christian groups and individuals in the first years of the Church. Finally there is a book which is different to all the others in the New Testament. It is called the Revelation of John and was written to help the early Christians keep their faith and persevere with the new life they had accepted as Christians.

"The New Testament is the specifically Christian part of the Bible. The beliefs it expresses about Jesus are not shared by Jews."

7
Beliefs and Doubts

Gary and his grandfather were joined by Mrs Thomas, Susan and Nina. Both girls had been studying religion at school and found it very interesting. There were often discussions in their class among people with totally different beliefs.

"Remember, Gary," continued Grandad Thomas, "Jesus was a Jew. He lived as a Jew, he went to the synagogue and all his followers were Jews, but he had come with a new message for the Jewish people. He taught that God's promises and the predictions made by the prophets in the Old Testament were about to be fulfilled. The Kingdom of God was about to arrive. Jesus said that a new age was coming, a time when everyone would live by God's rule."

"We haven't been told about the Kingdom of God at school," commented Gary. "We learn all about the birth of Jesus and how he performed miracles, like feeding thousands of people or turning water into wine."

"It was the same when I was at school," replied his grandfather. "The message Jesus brought is not as well known as the astonishing things that occurred in his lifetime."

"I like hearing about the miracles," put in Nina. "As you know, I'm a Hindu, and we have hundreds of stories about the amazing events that took place when our gods lived on earth. At school they are always called 'Hindu **myths** and legends', but when similar stories are told about Jesus everyone seems to accept them as fact."

Mrs Thomas asked Nina, "I wonder, Nina, do you believe

48

that all those stories about Hindu gods and goddesses are true, that they really happened?"

"No, not really. Some Hindus do believe them, but I think the stories have a message. They are meant to help us understand the truth. When we have a problem we ask ourselves, what would Lord Krishna do in this situation? We remember the things that happened to Krishna and how he reacted and then try to follow his example."

"Well, I think the stories written about Jesus really did happen," argued Gary. "Why would anyone make them up if they didn't?"

Grandad Thomas nodded in agreement. "Perhaps we do concentrate too much on the unusual events in Jesus's life, but I also believe that they happened."

"I'm not so sure," said Mrs Thomas. "The writers of the

The Feeding of the Five Thousand is the only miracle to be recorded in all four Gospels.

Gospels, Matthew, Mark, Luke and John, were all absolutely convinced that Jesus was the one the Jews had been waiting for, the **Messiah** promised by God. Other people had claimed to be the Messiah and most of them had been killed by the Romans. These four writers were certain that this time the real Messiah had arrived and they wanted to tell the world about him. The books they wrote about him are called Gospels, a word that means 'good news'. Many Christians accept that the Gospels were not written as history books but to explain to people the importance of Jesus's life and teachings.

"In our modern world when we hear about some important event we ask, 'How did it happen?'. Two thousand years ago the Jewish people would not have asked that question. Instead they would probably have asked, 'What does it mean?'. This was certainly the case when Jesus spoke in **parables**, which are stories used to explain religious ideas. After he had told a parable to a crowd of people, the parable of the sower, for example, the disciples often asked him to explain the meaning of the story."

"What you are saying, Mrs Thomas, is that the Gospels were written to explain the meaning behind the life of Jesus."

"That's right, Nina. Matthew wanted to show Jewish Christians what Jesus's life meant. He did not doubt that Jesus was the Messiah, and he wanted his readers to believe too."

"If the Jews had expected the Messiah to free them from the Romans and lead them to a new life, it must have been quite a shock for Jesus's early followers when he was crucified," said Susan.

"Let me put it this way," replied her mother. "If Nina came round and said she had tickets for a rock concert in Birmingham, you would have a picture in your mind of what to expect from the band, even though she hadn't told you their name. Imagine that when they came on stage they were all over fifty years old, bald, overweight and wearing pinstripe suits. What would you think?"

"Don't be daft, Mum. How could it be a rock band if they were like that?"

"I see what your mum's getting at, Susan," said Nina. "She means that young people have an idea of what to expect before they see a band play. Two thousand years ago the Jewish people had a clear idea of what to expect from a Messiah. If Jesus was the Messiah, Matthew had to convince them with his Gospel. How did he do it, Mrs Thomas?"

"Well, I'm not an expert on this subject, you know, but I have been to Bible classes and discussion groups, where we talk about these things. Let's look at the **Christmas** story. That may be one example of how Matthew tries to show that Jesus was the Messiah.

Neither John nor Mark include the story of Jesus's birth in their Gospels. Matthew's account recalls the biblical prophecy that the Messiah would be born in Bethelehem.

51

"Matthew knew that the Jewish prophets had forecast many things about the Messiah. For instance, they had predicted he would be descended from King David, so Matthew begins his Gospel with a family tree to show us that Jesus was descended from King David. Many people believed that the Old Testament prophet Isaiah had predicted the Messiah would be the son of a virgin. Matthew's story includes the fact that Mary was a virgin.

"The prophet Micah had forecast that the Messiah would be born in Bethlehem. Matthew reports that Jesus was born there. The prophet Hosea had prophesied that the Messiah would come from Egypt and be brought back to his own land only after the death of King Herod."

"So Matthew knew about these predictions, and he knew that other Jews would believe Jesus was the Messiah if they were convinced the predictions had come true," said Susan.

"Yes, that's what your mum thinks happened," said Grandad Thomas, "but I don't agree with her. As I see it, the Old Testament predicts the coming of Jesus. I think that the events Matthew describes prove that Jesus was the man promised by God and that God revealed to the prophets what to expect of his chosen one."

Mrs Thomas felt it was time to bring the discussion to an end, or they would be arguing all night!

"Your grandad believes that the Gospels are true histories of the life of Jesus. I have my doubts about that. What we don't disagree about is that Jesus was the Messiah. I don't worry too much about how and where he was born, or whether he could turn water into wine at weddings. The message Jesus brought is the most important thing in my life. I shall always try to follow his teaching and example."

"Up to now I'd always thought our two religions were completely different," said Nina. "Today I realized that the discussions my parents have about our Hindu gods are the same as those you have about your God. It makes me feel we have much more in common than I'd ever imagined."

SUGGESTIONS FOR FURTHER STUDY

1 Discuss with members of two different denominations or religions the ceremonies that mark their initiation into, or increased commitment to, their particular faith.

2 Compare the ceremonies that mark key points during a Christian's life with those that take place in other major religions. Find out where the ceremonies are held, the stage at which they occur, whether a priest or other religious leader is present and what promises (if any) are made.

3 The Bible is divided into books, chapters and verses. To make it easier to find a reference, abbreviations are used. For example, "Matthew's Gospel, Chapter 3, verse 21" becomes "Matt. 3:21". Look up Mark 1:16–20 and write down the names of the first disciples.

4 List the names of the twelve disciples and note down references for passages in the Bible that give information about each one.

5 Sometimes the writers of the Gospels wrote different versions of the same event. Look at these versions of the death of Jesus:
(a) John 19:25–30
(b) Mark 15:33–39
Which do you think is more likely to be a true description? Discuss this with your friends and give reasons for your opinion.

8
Activity Week

Every year the churches in the town combine for a week of Christian activity. The aim is to show people that the churches have a part to play in the life of the town. The churches always provide a range of activities open to all young people. The youth clubs have "open-door" sessions where admission is free and special events are arranged.

This year six live bands played at various clubs. A roller-disco marathon took place as well as the usual club activities. Every youth-club member did their best to bring along a friend. A special effort was made to invite people who didn't seem to have many friends and not much of a social life.

Gary and Susan's youth club decided to concentrate on local young people who had been in trouble with the police and who might avoid further trouble if they could find something interesting to do with their time. Susan knew many local teenagers who were just bored. They didn't want to stay at home with their families in the evening. They spent most of their time wandering around with friends. Sometimes to relieve the boredom they did things that most of them knew were stupid or dangerous.

Three people in Susan's class had been taken to court for breaking into a newsagent's and stealing cigarettes. Susan also knew of two girls who had been sniffing solvents. Knowing the risks they were running, she talked it over with one of the youth-club leaders.

Linda, the youngest of the leaders, was keen that Susan should invite the people she had mentioned. Geoff, a more experienced youthleader, was not so sure. He raised a question that he knew would come up sooner or later.

"Look, Linda, the parents of our regular members know that this youth club is well run. They know most of the other kids' families because they nearly all attend our church. Can we risk some of them taking their sons and daughters away from the club? They may do that if they hear we are inviting along people who have been involved in stealing or solvent abuse."

Linda was annoyed at Geoff, although she knew he had a point. She felt that the idea of inviting outsiders was worth fighting for.

"What are we here for, Geoff? We are a church youth club in the middle of a big town. If we have nothing to offer those outside our own church then we're not doing our job. I like all the kids who already come here and I don't want any of them to leave but we must do something for the ones who need help most. I say we ask all the members – let them decide. If they agree we'll let the parents know what we propose. I know the vicar will back us."

Geoff agreed and the case was presented to the other members of the club. Many of them wanted an opportunity to speak about the situation. A large number were not keen on the idea of inviting some of the people mentioned. One or two said it would lead to fights, others that their parents would stop them coming if they knew that kids who had been on glue might be allowed in. Susan decided to have her say.

"Do you remember when we were all raising money to help Peter Kennedy, not very long ago? He has gone abroad to work with people who really need him, rather than staying here among people who are as fortunate as himself. He said the job of a Christian is to help those who need you, whether they go to church or not. It also means helping those who behave in a way that we regard as wrong. You can't help people who need you by keeping them out of the club. Peter set us an example. I say we invite them along, ask them to join us. We have club rules, after all, and if they don't enjoy being with us they won't come back. I'm with Linda on this one. I think the vicar can persuade our parents to back us up. Surely it's worth a try?"

Sue waited for a response but none came. Eventually Geoff spoke.

"I guess we all know Susan's right. Let's not be selfish. OK, there's some planning to be done. Does everyone agree?"

Everyone did. The youth club would make the effort to involve outsiders.

It was decided to take some of the newcomers to the mountain centre that was being built in the Lake District. The local churches had clubbed together to buy a derelict sheep-farm high on a fell. Each year parties of young people went up to the farm to join in its rebuilding. The aim was to provide a holiday centre that could be used by all voluntary groups and schools in the town. It would be cheap to run and would provide a complete change from town life.

When the farm was bought, little remained of the original buildings. Volunteers had pitched tents near the farm and set to work preparing the site for the work that was to follow.

This was to be Susan's second trip to the farm. Linda and Geoff went every year. They used two minibuses for the journey. At weekends someone with a particular skill, such as roofing or plumbing, would be on hand to direct operations. The last time Susan went she had been involved in plumbing in a new water supply. Everyone took turns to do routine tasks like cooking, washing and cleaning as well as sharing the more challenging building work. Now the plumbing was complete, the roof had been restored and the gas lights and cooker were all connected up to the gas-bottles in the yard. The volunteers were to spend the week repairing drystone walls and constructing and fitting bunk-beds.

It was hard work. The stones were heavy and the weather had a nasty habit of changing from bright sunshine to heavy rain before the farm and cagoules could be reached.

As part of its wide-ranging welfare work, the Church Army runs several holiday centres. Here preparations are made for a new drama season at a rural centre with its own open-air theatre.

In the evenings work ended at seven o'clock. Usually they had a barbecue at eight o'clock and sat around the dying embers of the fire until long after the sun had set. They told stories and jokes, sang songs and enjoyed each other's company.

By the end of their stay all the volunteers had learned a great deal. They found it satisfying to work as a team, for others, and didn't mind how hard they had to work. The worst fears of the group had not been fulfilled. The young people invited to join the party had enjoyed it as much as the rest, and there had been no trouble. The only arguments were about who would get priority when the next visit was planned!

9
Sunday

The telephone rang. It was Nina, phoning to catch up on the news from the Lake District.

"We had a great time," Susan told her. "There was plenty of hard work to do, but we had some good fun as well. Do you remember Tracey Brooks? She left school last year."

"Oh, yes, her parents run the newsagent's in the High Street."

"Well, she came with us and really enjoyed herself. In fact, she wants to join the youth club, and she's coming to church with me today. She'll be round in about an hour."

"She must have enjoyed herself," answered Nina, "because she used to say religion was really boring."

"I know, but I told her you had come to the Easter service with us and that other visitors are quite common at our services. That seemed to encourage her. Would you like to come as well? I'm sure Tracey won't mind."

"I haven't anything planned for today. OK, I'll come."

The three girls arrived at the church just in time. The Thomases were already sitting near the front. There were about eighty people in the congregation and another twelve or so in the choir.

Susan had mentioned to her friends that there was to be an infant baptism as part of the Holy Communion service that morning.

The vicar entered and the service began. It was not long before Nina and Tracey felt the same sense of unity and sharing which they had both experienced before, Nina on the hillside on Easter Sunday and Tracey in the Lake District the previous week.

Two parts of the service particularly impressed Nina and Tracey. One was the way in which the baptism took place. As the child was too young to know what was happening, both the parents and the godparents promised Mr Rees that they would set a Christian example for the child to follow. The vicar then dipped his finger in the water in the font and traced the sign of the cross on the baby's forehead, saying, "Kevin Mark, I baptise you in the name of the Father, and of the Son, and of the Holy Spirit." Still speaking to the baby, Mr Rees continued, "God has received you by baptism into his Church." The congregation responded, "We welcome you into the Lord's Family."

The girls noticed that, although the baptism was a family event, the rest of the congregation seemed pleased to receive a new person into their Church.

The second part of the service that stuck in the girls' minds was when the vicar gave the bread and wine at the Communion-rail. Like the rest of the congregation, the three

Several babies are being baptized at this Anglican baptism ceremony. Note the simple, modern font.

Holy Communion

of them had gone to the rail and knelt down. When it was her turn, Susan, who had been confirmed two years earlier, received the bread and wine. Although they were not church members Mr Rees did not ignore Tracey and Nina. He said a short prayer for each of them and then continued giving Communion to the other worshippers. This made them feel very welcome.

After the service members of the congregation stopped to chat to each other. Everyone seemed very friendly.

On the way back to Susan's house Mrs Thomas invited Tracey and Nina to lunch. Nina didn't know whether she should accept. She knew that the food had been cooking in the oven while they were in church and she remembered what a big appetite Gary had. Mr Thomas assured her that there would be plenty of roast potatoes, chicken and

60

vegetables for everyone, including Gary. With that settled, Tracey and Nina rang their parents from the Thomases' house to say where they were.

After the meal the girls volunteered to help Mr Thomas with the washing-up.

"Wasn't the baby good this morning?" remarked Tracey. "He didn't even cry."

"Yes, he was," agreed Susan. "Do you remember when Jane Smith was baptized, Dad? She cried all the way through the service!"

"Yes, that was a shame, but I understand she's a good baby really."

"Do you only baptize babies in your church?" asked Tracey.

"Oh no," replied Mr Thomas. "Older children and adults can be baptized. The service is usually a little different. Mr Rees talks directly to the person being baptized as well as to the godparents, and obviously adults don't need god-parents."

"Why did the younger children leave the service before Communion this morning?" asked Nina.

"They went to Junior Church," answered Susan. "It's a bit like Sunday school, where they go to classes to learn more about Christianity and the Bible. Most of the children are too young to understand the sermon and Holy Communion, so Junior Church saves them getting bored."

"I always thought people dressed up in their best clothes to go to church, but that didn't seem to be the case today," said Tracey.

"Oh yes, I remember putting on my smartest clothes, my 'Sunday best', for church when I was younger," recollected Mr Thomas. "It's a little different now, at least in our church. Some people dress in suits but others prefer to wear their everyday clothes, like jeans and sweaters. In church, the vicar always wears a clerical collar and his **cassock**, the long black robe you saw him in today. In fact, he usually wears his clerical collar on weekdays too if he's on Church business."

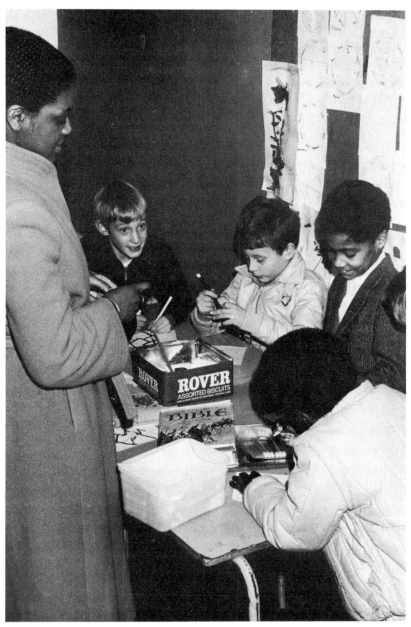

Junior Church

"What does Mr Rees do during the week?" enquired Tracey.

"He does a lot of visiting around his parish," replied Mr Thomas. "He goes to see a number of old-age pensioners and those who are ill, whether at home or in hospital, as well as visiting the local prison each week to talk to the inmates. He visits schools from time to time, and holds confirmation classes and church services on a regular basis. I understand he is also a member of one or two diocesan committees, so all in all he is very busy."

"Why is Sunday the special day for Christians?" Nina asked.

"Many religions have a special day during the week. For Muslims it's Friday, for Jews it's Saturday. Christians chose Sunday because it was the day of Jesus's resurrection. It has traditionally been a day of rest and prayer. Most shops, offices and factories are closed on Sundays so Christians have an opportunity to go to church.

"There's another service at church this evening. It's called Evensong, and it's shorter than this morning's service. There won't be a choir there. Mrs Thomas and I will go, but Susan and Gary may do some homework instead."

When they had finished the washing-up, Mr Thomas and the girls rejoined the others. Gary was talking about the church choir.

"It's never been the same since I left," he boasted.

"Don't you believe him," interrupted Susan. "It's just as good now. Anyway, Gary, they don't have 'croakers' in the choir. When your voice started breaking you couldn't reach all the notes without squeaking or croaking."

"All right, you two, we've got the message," laughed Mrs Thomas. "We seem to have talked a lot about church today. Would anyone like to do anything else?"

With that, the girls disappeared upstairs to listen to records and Gary went out on his bike. Mr and Mrs Thomas decided to go for a walk, leaving Grandad to doze off in front of the television.

10
School Visit

Susan's school, St Mary's, had been paired with Abbey House, a school in the next county. For most of the year they had been exchanging letters, examples of work and slides about their activities. Near the end of the summer term the staff arranged for Susan's class to visit Abbey House for a day.

When they arrived they were surprised by the contrast between the two buildings. St Mary's is a modern school, opened twenty years ago. Abbey House is much older, built of stone with wood-panelled corridors and class-rooms with very high ceilings.

A group of host pupils welcomed their visitors with a short talk about Abbey House before showing them around:

"This school has a long history dating back to the sixteenth century. In those days education in England was provided by the Church. During its early years the school educated only boys, most of whom were from quite wealthy families. A few poor children received scholarships which enabled them to attend. In those days the rich saw no reason for the poor to be educated. For almost four hundred years Abbey House has provided education for children from Church of England families and now has nine hundred pupils aged between eleven and eighteen."

During the morning the two classes took part in a number of activities, including a play and a netball match. At lunch-time Susan paired up with Lucy, her pen-friend. As they ate, the two girls discussed their schools.

Susan had been thinking about the introductory talk they had listened to that morning. "We learned about the education system last term," she told Lucy. "We found out how the Churches tried to educate the poor people in the eighteenth century so that they could read the Bible, and how the local squires and then the factory owners tried to stop them, because they wanted the children to work.

"Our teacher told us that at first education could be given only in Sunday schools because people worked on the other six days. Then, more and more Church day-schools opened in the towns. It wasn't until 1870 that the Government agreed to build schools where the Church couldn't provide them. That's why there are both Church schools and State schools in Britain today."

"Ragged school" for poor children, 1857. The teacher is Thomas Guthrie, a Scottish preacher who campaigned for education for all.

A question occurred to her. She asked Lucy whether it was true that Abbey House accepted only children who belonged to the Church of England.

"Oh, yes," replied Lucy. "There are quite a few schools in the area but you can't get into this one unless you go to church."

Susan was curious. "How do they know whether you go to church or not?"

"That's simple," said Lucy. "When you are ten and about to leave primary school your parents have to ask the vicar to sign a form saying that your family goes to church. That makes sure you get a place."

Susan looked surprised. "My school's run by the Church of England, too, but we don't have a system like yours. As you can see, there are Muslims and Hindus in my class. People of any culture or religious beliefs – or none at all – can go to St Mary's.

Vicar with children from a Church school at their Christmas party

"At our last Speech Day, the headteacher told us how he sees the role of a Church school. He said that the Church has a duty to work towards a society that lives together in harmony. In his opinion, it is harder to achieve that if children from different backgrounds and cultures are educated separately, so that they don't mix with people who have other ways of seeing the world. He thinks that the Church and its schools should help everyone, because that was one of Jesus's main messages."

"I understand all that," replied Lucy, "but how does it make your school any different from an ordinary State school? I mean, most schools are State schools and they educate pupils of all religions together."

"Well, the headteacher explained that the special feature of St Mary's was that the staff shared a belief in the purpose of education. He called it the 'ethos' of the school."

"What did he mean?"

"The way the teachers behave, how they treat people. Nearly all of them are practising Christians and their attitudes and behaviour reflect their beliefs. They try to be fair and to make us think about other people's needs and problems. The head made it clear that being a Christian means serving others through your work. We see the teachers at prayer in the school chapel and we know that they also respect the beliefs of others although they may not share them."

"I don't think my parents would agree with those ideas," said Lucy. "They think that my school should give me a Christian education. It should teach me about Jesus and his life and about what **Anglicans** believe. They say that because the Church of England pays some of the costs of the building, and because the money comes from Church members, Anglicans should have first choice of places at the school. That seems fair to me."

The two girls, both of the same age and both at Church schools, agreed to differ about the role of Church schools in the community.

SUGGESTIONS FOR FURTHER STUDY

1 Are any churches in your area involved in projects designed to help others? If so, write an account of at least one such project, illustrated with your own drawings.

2 How would you and your friends react if you were members of a youth club like Susan's and faced the same situation? Would you agree with Susan or vote to keep out possible trouble-makers?

3 Sunday is the special day for Christians, Friday for Muslims and Saturday for Jews. (The Jewish Shabbat, or Sabbath, starts at sunset on Friday and ends at sunset on Saturday, while the Muslim "day of congregation" begins at sunset on Thursday and ends at sunset on Friday.) Why do religions have a special day? Contact Jewish, Christian or Muslim members of your community to find out how they spend their special day.

4 The number of services held in one week varies from church to church. Record the pattern of services at three or four local churches.

5 Trace the history of schools in your area using old maps, town directories and school log-books if you can borrow them. Find out how old your school is and which schools served the area in the past. Are there any Church schools near by? To which denomination do they belong?

6 Find out whether there are any Muslim, Jewish or other non-Christian schools in your area. Discuss whether it is a good thing for people of different faiths to be educated separately.

7 When did Sunday schools begin in Britain? Name some of the people who played a part in the early history of the Sunday-school movement.

11
Death of a Friend

Gary's friend Liam had been ill for a long time. At first he seemed to feel tired when everyone else had lots of energy. Later he complained of terrible aches and pains after playing football or joining in a P.E. lesson.

Gary had sometimes lost his temper with his friend. "Why not pack up playing, Liam? You moan after every match. We all get kicked and bruised but the rest of us just get on with the game. We're all tired of you and your moaning. You're no fun any more."

It was soon after Gary had said those words that Liam began to miss school. The absences grew longer and Gary suspected there was something seriously wrong with his friend.

Gary's worst fears were confirmed when his mother broke the news to him one Saturday morning. "Gary, you know Liam's been ill for a long time. The doctors are now certain he's got a form of leukaemia. They've tried different treatments but he's not responding. His mum says he probably hasn't more than three or four weeks to live."

"I'd guessed it was something like that, Mum, the way no one wanted me to visit. I would like to see Liam if I can. I might be able to cheer him up."

"I'm sure you could, Gary. We didn't want you to go because he looks so different, and we thought you might be upset. He isn't going to get better, though. Are you sure you want to go?"

Gary was quite sure. "We've been friends for years, Mum. I have to go – what kind of friend do you think I am?"

Gary's visit lasted nearly an hour. Liam looked very ill and tired. He was much thinner and he had lost most of his hair. Gary told Liam all the news from school – about the time when the history teacher fell asleep in assembly, about who was in trouble with which teacher, and which boys liked which girls. Liam enjoyed the visit. His eyes seemed to light up as Gary described the day-to-day details of school life. When he left, Gary promised to call again the following week.

Gary did not make the next visit. Four days later his friend died. Even though Gary knew it was going to happen he couldn't believe it. He tried to keep his feelings under control but as soon as he was in his own room he felt the tears begin to roll down his cheeks. He couldn't help himself.

The funeral was arranged for the following Tuesday. A service was held for Liam in the church at 10.15. Gary's family were all there, as were many of Liam's school-friends and some of his teachers.

There were prayers and two hymns, but Gary couldn't sing. He felt as though he had an enormous lump in his throat. The vicar spoke about Liam and how difficult it was to understand how someone so young could be taken from his family.

At the end of the service the coffin was placed in the **hearse**. Liam's family followed in the funeral cars and the other members of the congregation drove to the **crematorium** in their own cars.

A few words were spoken at the crematorium before the blue curtains closed around the coffin. Liam's family left the crematorium in tears. Many others were very upset.

Gary was glad to get out into the fresh air again. Some of the words from the service kept coming into his mind: "Forasmuch as it hath pleased Almighty God of his great mercy to take unto himself the soul of our dear Liam here departed ... in sure and certain hope of the resurrection to eternal life."

All the mourners were invited back to Liam's house. Gary

Hearse and mourners outside a crematorium

didn't know what to say to the people there. The table was piled high with sandwiches and cakes, there was a trolley loaded with cups of tea and some of the adults were drinking sherry.

"Mum, I've got to talk to you." Gary needed to get something off his chest. "Why is there all this food and drink? Look at everyone – it's like a party!"

"A funeral is a difficult event for the family and friends, Gary. They're full of emotions that they can't understand or control. They will have to express their grief and come to terms with their loss, but for the moment they need something to do. That's why this special meal helps. It would be no good everyone coming here to stare at each other – imagine the feelings of the family then. Now they are all busy, and yet Liam's death is being marked by a gathering of family and friends who share in the sadness and will keep his memory."

Mrs Thomas knew Gary had something else on his mind.

"Gary, I don't understand how God can allow something like this to happen, either. I know that many Christians would say he has been chosen to be with God, or that God doesn't control our everyday lives – because if he did we wouldn't be free – but those explanations don't take away the pain. When something like this happens we look to God for a miracle. What I do know is that through our faith in Jesus we can all help Liam's family.

"We believe that when Jesus died it was not the end of his existence. His resurrection gave him a new life with God, and his death gave all those who believe in him the same chance of a new life. Liam's death is not the end, although he is no longer with us. He is already with Jesus and he is living again. We can look forward to the day when we will join Liam and Jesus. Does that thought help?"

"I suppose it helps a bit, but there's something else that's worrying me. I never told you this, Mum, but just before Liam was absent from school I told him I was fed up with his moaning. I told him he was no fun any more. When I went to see him I wanted to apologize, but I couldn't. I was determined to do it on my next visit but he died – I never made that visit. Now he'll never know I was sorry."

"Gary, we all say things we regret. At times like this we realize how hurtful we can be to other people. Maybe this is a lesson to all of us not to say hurtful things to people, but I know Liam didn't need you to apologize. Actions are more important than words. When you knew he was ill you didn't think twice. You went round there and brought him a little happiness at his worst moments. That would be his final memory of you, Gary – not a few cross words spoken when you were in a bad mood. Now come on, make yourself useful. There are people here who need cheering up. Let's go and help them."

12
An Old Church

Mr and Mrs Thomas were pleased that their family holiday on the farm was going well. They had been a little worried beforehand that there would not be enough for Susan and Gary to do, but that certainly did not seem to be the case. Besides spending time at the farm and helping with the animals, they had visited local museums, a country park, a gymkhana and an air display. Today they were going to the church fête.

Mr and Mrs Thomas spent a lot of time talking to Mr Howard, the vicar, at the fête. Realizing that the village church was much older than their own church, St Martin's, they arranged to have a look around it the following day. Mr Howard said he would be happy to meet them all in the morning and tell them a little about the church's history.

Susan and Gary were very interested in what Mr Howard had to say. He explained that churches had nearly always been built in the centre of the towns or villages they served. This made it easier for people to attend the services. His church, St James's, was no exception.

Churches have been built in Britain for hundreds of years, but very few of the oldest ones are still standing. Some of the early buildings were built out of wood and have rotted away. Others, made out of stone, were pulled down and the stone has been used again for other building work. A few buildings dating back fifteen hundred years to Celtic times are still standing. These are very simple, small structures, but they are proof that groups of Christians lived here long ago.

Saxon and particularly Norman churches are quite common in Britain.

"Is there a way of knowing when a church was first built?" Susan asked Mr Howard. "Can you tell by the type of stone the builders used?"

"No, it isn't that simple, I'm afraid. You see, a church made of granite will last for centuries, but a sandstone church will soon look old and crumbling. Builders simply used the most readily available local stone. Some types of stone last longer than others. The best way to tell the age of a building is from its style. Churches are a little like clothes: fashions keep changing. Sometimes it's because builders develop new methods, but often it's simply that one style replaces another as the most popular."

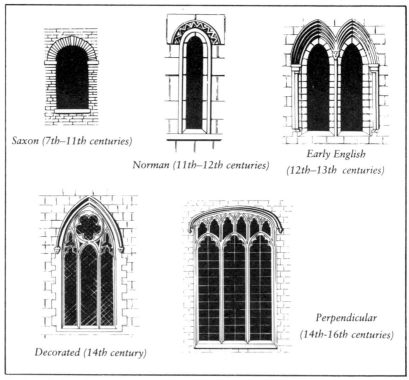

Saxon (7th–11th centuries)

Norman (11th–12th centuries)

Early English (12th–13th centuries)

Decorated (14th century)

Perpendicular (14th–16th centuries)

Styles of church windows

Mr Howard took the Thomas family into the vestry and showed them a book containing drawings of the changing styles of British churches. Next to the drawings were dates showing when a particular style was popular. He pointed out that such dates are a useful guide but because building styles change gradually some designs may overlap at certain times.

"How old is this church?" asked Gary.

"The earliest parts date from Norman times. You can tell that by some of the windows. The church was extended later as the village grew in size. A few of the older churches have certain interesting features. Whenever you visit an old church, see if it has a pillory or stocks – once used for punishing petty criminals – or a tithe-barn."

"What is a tithe-barn?"

"A building where tithes were stored. A tithe is one tenth of a person's income. People used to pay tithes to the vicar, either in cash or, more commonly, in kind: animals or farm produce, for instance. Quite a few old churches, like St James's, have a lych-gate. This is where the coffin was rested while the vicar began the burial service."

"Even when they have different features outside, most churches look quite similar inside," observed Susan. "For instance, you usually walk along an aisle to an altar at the far end."

"Interesting you should say that, because most churches do follow that plan. There is a reason for it. Nearly all churches are built with the altar at the east end. The congregation either stand or sit facing the altar. Many churches are even built in the shape of a cross. Christians believe that Jesus will keep his promise to return to us. Churches were usually built facing east because that is the direction people expected Jesus to come from.

"They would also place a beautiful stained-glass window in the east wall. When the sun shone through it the church would be filled with coloured light. Many stained-glass windows show scenes from the Bible. As the sun rises on a spring morning its rays shine through the picture, filling the church with coloured light. It's a beautiful sight, and it reminds the worshippers of Jesus's promise to return to earth.

"For the same reason, most Christians are traditionally buried in the church graveyard with their feet to the east, so that if Jesus returned they would be facing him. Now, follow me and we'll go back into the aisles and have a good look around."

"This church is very different from ours," remarked Susan. "St Martin's doesn't have a graveyard. There isn't enough room for one with all the houses around it. It's a modern building built out of brick, not stone, the pews aren't fixed to the floor and it has fitted carpets."

"You will no doubt find our stone flagged floor very cold then."

"What is that wooden screen for?" asked Gary.

"The screen is a clue which tells us something about how people used to worship. You know that nowadays the whole congregation is involved in the service. Everyone can see what is going on, and they all say the prayers. In many churches the worshippers discuss the types of prayers and hymns they want to use for their kind of worship. We have Junior Church for the young people, members of the congregation read from the Bible and all the adults may come to the altar to receive Communion. In the past none of this would have happened.

"Until the 1500s a church was divided into two separate sections. The **chancel**, at the eastern end, contained the altar. This part of the chancel was called the sanctuary. Only the priests and his assistants were allowed to enter it. The congregation remained in the **nave** while the vicar celebrated the **Eucharist** in the sanctuary. In many churches they could only hear the vicar, because he was hidden by the screen that separated the nave from the chancel. Sometimes the screen (called a **rood-screen**) was even locked to keep the congregation away from the altar. Some churches, like St James's, still have rood-screens today. As you can see, these

76

Pictures of saints on a rood-screen defaced in the sixteenth century

contain some of the most magnificent wood-carving ever produced in Britain.

"Do you see that statue of Jesus on the cross above the screen? That is known as the **rood**. On either side of the rood there used to be statues of the Virgin Mary and St John. Before the sixteenth century the rood was one of the most important parts of the church. There was a lamp in front of it, it was decorated at festival times and the ceiling above was highly decorated. Many of these statues were destroyed in the sixteenth and seventeenth centuries. In some churches, like St James's, we can still see the rood-beams on which the rood stood and the rood-stairs which led to it. Although ours has been destroyed, the rood-loft (a gallery on top of the rood-screen) is still preserved in some churches."

"Why were so many churches damaged during the sixteenth century?" enquired Susan.

77

"Well, if you don't mind a bit more history, I'll explain. During the early 1600s the most powerful group of people in the country were known as Puritans. They believed that Christianity should be practised much as it had been in the early years of the religion. They felt that there should be no place for bishops and archbishops and that each local congregation should control its own church and form of worship, meeting representatives of other districts at assemblies.

"The Puritans were against special clothing for ministers and wanted to get rid of most of the decoration, statues and symbols found in churches. They also believed it was their duty to simplify church services. They set about destroying those things they disliked. For instance, a great deal of beautiful stained glass in churches was damaged beyond repair. That is why even in old churches like this one some of the stained glass is not very old. Statues were smashed, crosses knocked down and screens destroyed. The brightly coloured wall-paintings decorating some churches were whitewashed over. Altars made of stone were damaged, too. Nowadays most altars are made of wood, like the altars used by the early Church, and are simple in appearance. They have only one cross instead of the five found on many altars until the seventeenth century."

"Yes, the altar at our church is a wooden one. It's much smaller than yours," remarked Susan.

When entering the church Gary had noticed some ropes hanging down. They appeared to come from inside the church tower. As St Martin's did not have a tower he was pleased when Mr Howard began to explain.

"Towers are built to hold bells. The sound of bells can be heard all around and is a signal that a service is about to start. You should remember that until this century there was no TV or radio and few people read newspapers. In the past if there was an important announcement to be made, the church bells were rung to call the people together. They were also rung to warn of fire or attack. Some towers were used to

Bell taken down from the tower for repair

79

defend the church against attackers. Many new churches are built without spires or towers."

Susan had noticed the ornate stone font at the west end of the nave. "This is a much bigger font than the one at our church," she said.

"Yes, modern fonts are usually quite small and neat. That is because these days we Anglicans use only a little holy water on the forehead of the person being baptized. Some old fonts, like this one, are quite large. In Saxon times adults used to stand in them to be baptized, so they needed to be big."

Remembering his friend Paul, Gary said that this sounded similar to the way some Baptists are baptized today.

Mrs Thomas admired the detailed carvings on the **pulpit**. Mr Howard told her that theirs was believed to be one of the earliest examples of a pulpit. It dated back to the 1500s, when pulpits were first used in churches.

Ornate brass lectern   *Font with Norman bowl*

"We are very proud of both our old pulpit and our **lectern**. As you can see, the part of the lectern where the minister rests the service book is in the form of an eagle, carved out of wood. Modern ones are usually much plainer."

Gary had been wandering around the church looking at the cloth coverings on the altar, lectern and so on. He noticed that the letters IHS and I.N.R.I. occurred on a number of these. Although he had seen them before he did not know what they stood for, so he decided to ask Mr Howard.

"The New Testament was written in Greek. The first three letters of 'Jesus' are IHS in Greek. When Jesus was killed the Romans mocked him, and called him 'Jesus of Nazareth, King of the Jews'. In Latin this is written *Iesus Nazarenus Rex Iudaeorum*. That is where the initials I.N.R.I. come from."

The vicar then showed the Thomas family the church plate. There was a chalice which held the wine during Communion, a **paten** on which the bread was placed and two **alms** dishes which were used for collecting money during the services. They were all made of silver and looked valuable. At the Thomases' church there are similar objects but they are much plainer in style and certainly much less expensive.

Next Mr Howard pointed out the church chest. He told them that many of the records now kept by the Government or by the local Council were once the responsibility of the Church.

"The vicar used to have the task of recording every birth, baptism, marriage and death that took place in his parish. All of these were entered in the parish records, which were kept in a large chest like this one. I've also found wills, details of the vicar's activities, charity records and even weather reports in this chest! Some of them date back to the sixteenth century. The chest once contained the vicar's **vestments** as well as the records. Historians often depend on parish records to give them information about the past, but anyone may read them if they wish."

81

"You mentioned vestments," said Susan. "That reminded me of something Mr Rees, our vicar, told us. He said that long ago vestments used to be decorated with precious stones."

"That's quite right. Come into the vestry again and I'll show you some jewels and decorations we think were used on vestments hundreds of years ago. Some of the decorations are made of gold, so they're quite valuable. No doubt you've guessed that it was the Puritans who put a stop to decorated vestments. In fact, they wouldn't allow vestments to be worn at all. Now we wear them again, but without the jewels."

While they were in the vestry Mr Howard showed the Thomases the different-coloured **stoles** he wears around his neck and the different altar coverings used in the church according to the time of year. The colour violet, for example, is used during Lent and Advent, because violet is the colour of penitence; red, the colour of fire, is used at Whitsuntide, and white – for joy – at Christmas.

Vicar preaching from a pulpit

Gary was beginning to feel restless at being indoors when it was such a hot, sunny day. He thought of a way to steer the conversation.

"Why does your church have those ugly carvings on the outside?" he asked innocently.

Mr Howard looked puzzled, then laughed. "You mean the gargoyles! Let's go and have a look at them." He led the way outside.

Squinting in the strong sunlight, the Thomases gazed up at the gargoyles.

"As you've probably guessed, they are waterspouts," said Mr Howard. "They drain all the rainwater that falls on the church roof and throw it well away from the walls. There are a number of possible reasons why they represent such fearsome creatures. They are a warning to those entering the church to stop thinking evil thoughts, and they may have been images of hell, meant to frighten those who disobeyed the Church's teaching. Also, people used to believe that there

Cathedral stonemason working on a gargoyle

83

were strange invisible demons in the air that would attack churches. They hoped the gargoyles would keep those evil spirits away."

"Our church has football and cricket teams, a youth club, a coffee bar, Scouts and Guides as well as services. Is it the same at St James's?" asked Susan.

"Well, we're not quite so busy," smiled the vicar. "I said earlier that a church was usually built in the centre of a town or village. What goes on in any church reflects what its members want. Your parents told me that your church is situated in a busy town. The services it provides are those which its members want. Because St James's is in a small village with a rural community, we don't have a large congregation, although the majority of the villagers do attend. There aren't many children or teenagers in the village so we don't put on as many activities as your church does."

"You mentioned that the majority of villagers attend church," remarked Mrs Thomas. "That is certainly not the case in most towns, where the congregations are generally becoming smaller."

"Yes, but I mustn't create the wrong impression. It is true to say that Anglican churches are better supported in villages but even here congregations aren't what they used to be. For instance, many of us vicars look after more than one country parish. I look after this parish, St James's, as well as the neighbouring one, St Simon's. That means twice as many services on a Sunday in addition to all the other parish duties."

"That must keep you extremely busy," said Mr Thomas.

With that the Thomas family thanked the vicar for his time and for making their visit so interesting. For his part, Mr Howard said he had enjoyed showing them the church.

13
Marriage

"I don't know what my father will say about it," said Mrs Thomas. "I don't mind, but my family have always had strong views about this sort of thing."

"What are you talking about, Mum?" asked Gary.

"Oh, you must have heard by now, Gary. Your Aunt Christine is getting married."

"Why should Grandad Finch object? She is twenty-seven. You were married at twenty!"

"It's not her age, Gary, it's the fact that she's marrying a Roman Catholic that will bother him."

"You know, Mum, there seems to be a lot of fuss about Catholics marrying **Protestants**. Anyone would think that Catholics had two heads! They're Christians, aren't they?"

"Of course they are, but Roman Catholicism is a different denomination. Let me explain."

Mrs Thomas told Gary that until the 1500s the majority of Christians in Britain had accepted the **pope** as head of the Church. All the Christians of Western Europe belonged to the same Church. However, some people began to question the way Christianity was developing. Arguments raged about what it meant to be a Christian. As a result, the Christians of Western Europe divided into a number of major groups. The largest groups were the Roman Catholics and the Protestants.

The Catholics continued to regard the pope as leader of the Church, but the Protestants did not. (The Protestants took their name from the followers of Martin Luther, who "protested" in 1529 when they were no longer allowed to organize their own Church.) In 1534 King Henry VIII declared himself Head of the Church of England, and since then Britain has been a country where the majority of Christians are called Protestants.

There are many different groups of Protestants: Anglicans, Methodists, Baptists, Pentecostals and others. For many years it was illegal for Roman Catholics to worship in Britain but the law was changed in 1791, so now the Roman Catholic Church is also an important denomination in this country.

The largest of the Protestant Churches in Britain is the Anglican Church, the Church of England. There are great differences even within the Anglican denomination. Some of their churches are very ornate, others very simple.

Most of the other Protestant groups are known as **Nonconformist Churches**, "Nonconformist" because they objected to certain teachings of the Church of England and chose not to conform to them. The Nonconformists include the Methodist, Baptist, United Reformed and Pentecostal Churches. Generally speaking, their churches are simpler and plainer than those of the Church of England, and are often called **chapels**, to distinguish them from Anglican parish churches. They don't have bishops or **archbishops** in the way that Catholics and Anglicans do. Some Nonconformist Churches have male and female **ministers** but the Catholics and the Church of England have only male **priests**. Anglican priests can marry, whereas Catholic priests must remain single.

These days Christians try to concentrate on the things they have in common rather than on their differences. Many of the Churches in Britain belong to an organization called the British Council of Churches (B.C.C.). Through the B.C.C. they are members of the World Council of Churches (W.C.C.). The symbol of the W.C.C. is a ship and a cross with the word "*Oikoumene*" above. This is a Greek word meaning "world-wide". This coming together of the Churches is known as the **ecumenical** movement.

Woman minister of the United Reformed Church

Gary thought the ecumenical movement was a sensible idea. "It doesn't seem to have affected Grandad Finch much, though, does it, Mum?"

"No, there are people like your grandfather who aren't too happy about the ecumenical movement. They remember their childhood, when Protestants and Catholics went to separate schools and learned about how their ancestors were burned and tortured for their beliefs. In the town where Grandad lived there were two football teams, one supported by Protestants, the other by Catholics. When people left school Protestants were employed in certain industries and Catholics in others. The town was divided and there was a great deal of suspicion and dislike."

"Was this in Ireland?"

"No, Gary, in England. It's no longer like that in his home town but some of Grandad's views were formed when he was young and he still holds them, including the idea that Protestants shouldn't marry Catholics. He'd rather Christine married an atheist than a Roman Catholic, I think!"

The Archbishop of Canterbury, Dr Robert Runcie, celebrates the Eucharist with clergy of various denominations at the Sixth Assembly of the World Council of Churches in Vancouver, 1983.

88

Grandad Finch was not as difficult as Mrs Thomas had expected. Grandma Finch had already told him his ideas belonged to days which were better forgotten. She also made it clear she would not have her youngest daughter's happiness spoiled by any bad feeling.

The Thomas family arrived at Grandad and Grandma Finch's home the day before the wedding. Susan went with Christine to the travel agent's to collect her plane tickets; Graham and Christine would be flying to Dubrovnik for their honeymoon. On the way into town, Susan asked Christine where she and Graham had met.

"Well, we were both on a charity collection for Christian Aid, as representatives of our churches. We've been engaged for eighteen months but we both still spend a lot of our time working for Christian charities."

"Why did you decide on a church wedding? A lot of people I know get married in the register office."

"We thought about a register office wedding but decided that our marriage should be more than a legal contract. We

Inter-denominational gathering in Canterbury, 1984. From left: Sister Marion Eva (R.E. teacher), Cardinal Basil Hume, Pastor Io Smith (Leyton New Testament Assembly), Dr Robert Runcie and the Revd Sparkes (Baptist Union).

wanted our wedding to take the form of a religious service reminding us of our Christian responsibilities: that we are becoming as one and that we are entering a lifelong contract. We believe our vows are also taken in the presence of God. The legal part of the ceremony, the signing of the marriage register, is only one aspect of the service."

One of the main reasons for the increasing popularity of register office weddings is that a growing number of Christians are being divorced and wish to remarry. Some churches will marry divorced people, others won't. Priests who believe that marriage is for life will not marry divorced people. If Christians attend such a church they will usually remarry in a register office, but most churches will bless the couple in a church service after the wedding.

The following day Christine and her father arrived at the church in the wedding car just before 11 a.m. Grandad Finch took Christine by the arm and led her into the church and up the **aisle**, where Graham was waiting with the best man.

All four stood facing the vicar, Mr Bray. The vicar asked, "Who gives this woman to be married to this man?" and Grandad Finch passed Christine's hand to him.

Susan thought it didn't seem quite right that Christine appeared to be given by one man to another, but she decided not to say anything in case she was accused of spoiling things.

The vicar put Christine's right hand into Graham's and both partners exchanged vows:

"I, Graham (Christine), take you, Christine (Graham), to be my wife (husband), to have and to hold, from this day forward; for better, for worse, for richer, for poorer, in sickness and in health, to love, cherish, and worship, till death do us part, according to God's holy law; and this is my solemn vow."

Graham placed a ring on the fourth finger of Christine's left hand, saying, "With this ring I thee wed". Christine gave Graham a ring too.

Mr Bray pronounced them man and wife and, after a short

Confetti is thrown over the bride and groom as they leave the church.

address about the meaning and purpose of marriage, led them to the **vestry** to sign the marriage register.

In the afternoon everyone enjoyed a splendid meal at a nearby hotel and there was a disco that evening which went on until the early hours of the morning. Christine and Graham left for the airport at nine o'clock. Gary and Susan performed the traditional prank of tying boots, cans and balloons to the car.

"When I get married I'm going on my honeymoon by bus, then no one will be able to mess up my car," said Gary.

"Who'll marry you?" laughed Susan. "I don't think you've much chance to start with, but when you tell your girlfriend you're planning a honeymoon on a bus she won't stay around long! Come on, let's get back to the disco. You can buy me a Coke."

SUGGESTIONS FOR FURTHER STUDY

1 Liam was cremated, but in the past most people in Britain were buried. Visit your local cemetery with a parent or teacher and examine the headstones on the graves, particularly those dating from the nineteenth century and earlier. How old were the people buried there when they died? Now read the "deaths" column in your local newspaper. Compare the ages at which people die today with the ages you recorded in the cemetery. Can you suggest reasons for the difference between them?

2 Have you ever said things (to your parents, perhaps, or to a close friend) you later regretted? Were you able to apologize? Write about such an occasion and explain how you feel about it now.

3 Church leaders often wear special clothes. Find out as much as you can about the clothes worn by
(a) an Anglican or Roman Catholic archbishop
(b) an Anglican or Roman Catholic bishop
(c) an Anglican or Roman Catholic priest
(d) a Nonconformist minister (e.g. a Baptist)

4 Choose three different Christian denominations and find out all you can about their origins, beliefs, buildings and forms of worship. By visiting churches and chapels and talking to the clergy you will be able to add a great deal to what you read about each denomination.

5 Just as there are different denominations within the Christian Church, so there are divisions within most of the major religions of the world. For instance, there are Orthodox and Reform Jews, Theravada and Mahayana Buddhists and Sunni and Shiah Muslims. Choose two groups of believers from the same faith and give examples

of ways in which their beliefs and practices (a) differ and (b) are the same.

6 Find out how the marriage ceremony is carried out in another Christian denomination and compare it with the wedding described in Chapter 13.

7 Describe the marriage ceremony and traditions of a major religion other than Christianity. Make a list of the differences and the similarities between the wedding you study and a Christian wedding.

14
Christmas

Mrs Thomas was half expecting the request she received from Susan at the end of November.

"Mum, you remember last Easter when Nina came to stay? You must admit it was great having her with us. Well, I was wondering...."

"I know just what you were wondering," replied Mrs Thomas, "and I've already discussed it with your dad. Yes, Nina is very welcome to spend Christmas with us if she wants to."

Susan had brought up the subject on the way home from church. It was an appropriate moment because it was the first Sunday of **Advent**. "Advent" comes from a Latin word meaning "to come". It is the season in the Church year when Christians prepare for the celebration of the birth of Jesus. The first day of Advent is the fourth Sunday before Christmas Day.

On the first of December Mrs Thomas pinned the family Advent calendar on the kitchen wall. Gary and Susan had enjoyed opening the twenty-four windows on the calendar when they were younger, but for some time now they had regarded Advent calendars as childish. Mrs Thomas didn't mind – she enjoyed all the traditions associated with Christmas and if no one else wanted to open the windows, she would do it herself. As it happened, she often found the day's window already open when she got round to doing it. She didn't know who was responsible – it could even have been Mr Thomas!

The first task of Christmas had been completed at the beginning of November, seven weeks before Christmas. On the first Sunday afternoon in November the whole family gathered in the kitchen for "Christmas cake preparations" — what Mr Thomas called "the ritual".

Each member of the family took turns to mix and stir the ingredients. Gary and Susan usually argue about who should scrape out the mixing-bowl, but Susan now thought that was beneath her dignity, so Gary had it all to himself, much to his delight.

Mrs Thomas baked the cake and then wrapped it in foil and stored it in a tin to mature. Just before Christmas it would be iced and decorated.

On 21 December Nina went round to the Thomases' house. That evening, they all wrapped up well in warm coats, woolly hats and gloves. Mr Thomas gave Nina a torch to carry. They were off to join other members of the church in an evening of carol-singing around the parish. The leader of

Carol-singers in Birmingham

the Scout pack had an accordion and some of the Guides played their recorders. Many of Susan's and Gary's friends from the youth club were there.

The party toured the neighbourhood, stopping once or twice in each street to sing a different **Christmas carol**. The fittest members of the party ran from door to door inviting people to come out to listen, to join in if they wished, and to donate some money to the collection. All the money was for charity. Almost everyone seemed pleased to hear the carol-singers. People in Britain, whether or not they go to church, enjoy the traditions of Christmas and like to enter into the Christmas spirit.

Nina thoroughly enjoyed herself. She knew most of the carols from school and liked to sing them as much as anyone else.

The group arrived at the church hall at 10 p.m. They were beginning to feel tired and their throats were certainly a bit croaky, but they cheered up when they saw the rows of steaming hot drinks, mince pies and hot dogs awaiting them in the hall.

Different volunteers would go out singing carols on each night of the two weeks leading up to Christmas. In that way everyone in the parish could be sure that the church members would visit their street.

Mr and Mrs Thomas let Gary and Susan choose their main Christmas presents in advance, but on Christmas Day each member of the family receives a surprise present. As Nina was a guest it was important that she should not be left out.

Nina arrived at the Thomases around 8 p.m. on Christmas Eve. Susan and Gary had decorated the house with tinsel, holly and shiny streamers, and Gary was just putting the finishing touches to the Christmas tree. "The tree looks lovely," Nina complimented him.

Gary looked smug. "Of course – what else do you expect, with my talents?"

"Don't make him any more big-headed than he already is, Nina," warned Susan.

96

Choosing Christmas trees. For Christians, the fir (like holly and other evergreen plants) symbolizes eternal life.

Nina could see that the Thomases had made a lot of preparations for Christmas, including a log fire. "I've never seen a log fire before," she said, warming her hands.

"We always have one at Christmas. Dad makes a special effort to saw and split enough logs to last until Boxing Day."

The fire had died down by the time they left for the Christmas Eve service. It was quite a short Communion service, beginning at 11.30 p.m. and ending just after midnight.

"I suppose there will be a number of Christian services to attend at such an important time of the year," remarked Nina.

"Yes, there are always services on Christmas Day as well," answered Susan, "but we won't be going."

Before they went to bed, Nina said jokingly to Mr Thomas, "The last time I stayed here for a Christian festival I had to be up at five o'clock. Is it the same tomorrow?"

"No, Nina," Mr Thomas smiled. "You can sleep till seven o'clock. Then you must get up, because we all have to be out by eight."

"Mr Thomas – you're not serious, are you?"

"I'm afraid so, Nina. Tomorrow we leave at eight o'clock for the Central Methodist Hall. Volunteers from all the town's churches will be there. We'll be taking part in a rather unusual Christmas dinner."

As it happened, there was no need for Mrs Thomas to wake Nina. Gary's surprise present was a box of jokes and tricks. He woke Nina and Susan soon after six and proceeded to show them conjuring tricks, most of which went wrong.

Everyone had exchanged presents and eaten breakfast by a quarter to eight. They arrived at the Methodist Hall at eight o'clock.

"What exactly are we doing here?" asked Nina.

"Well, Nina," answered Mr Thomas, "do you know the Christmas story? You remember that Joseph and Mary arrived in Bethlehem with nowhere to stay. They went from inn to inn until they were finally given space in a stable, where Jesus was born.

"For many years, after attending a morning service on Christmas Day, we used to spend the whole day at home with our relatives. One day we saw a video at church about the homeless people of Britain. Mrs Thomas and I couldn't believe our eyes. We had no idea so many people live and sleep rough. When we heard that there are many homeless people in this town we decided we ought to do something about it. Representatives of all the local churches held a meeting and agreed to help homeless people in the town. The main thing we decided was that no one should be alone and hungry on Christmas Day.

"All the money we collected by carol-singing has been spent on today's celebrations. Homeless and hungry people know they can come to the Central Hall from 10 a.m. They can have hot showers, and the men can shave in hot water.

Christmas meal at a Salvation Army Goodwill Centre

There are Christmas presents for everyone as well as second-hand coats, shoes and clothes donated by local people."

Nina helped Susan and Gary to peel potatoes for the roasting-tin. Mrs Thomas was in charge of the Christmas puddings and Mr Thomas had to make sure that all the volunteers as well as the homeless were kept supplied with hot tea.

The highlight of the day was at noon, when all the people who had come to the Hall sat down to enjoy their Christmas dinner. Beforehand they had sung carols and been entertained by a comedian and a folk-singer. Most of all, though, they enjoyed the food, the warmth of the hall and the good company. It was three o'clock by the time the Thomases left. They were replaced by other church members, who had come to clear up the Hall.

Now the Thomas family could relax. Grandad and Grandma Thomas had invited them over for a family Christmas tea and supper.

Nina was very impressed by the way the house was decorated. A large Christmas tree stood in the corner, there were trimmings in every room and one wall was covered with Christmas cards from friends and relations.

Nina asked Mrs Thomas what all of this had to do with the Christmas story which she knew so well.

"Perhaps, Nina, you remember that when you were with us at Easter we discussed many of the traditions associated with that festival. Some of them dated from long before the time of Jesus and weren't strictly Christian. The same is true of Christmas."

Mrs Thomas explained that winter festivals, which marked the end of the old year and the start of the new, had been in existence for thousands of years. In Mesopotamia, four thousand years ago, a twelve-day festival was always held at about Christmas time. Two thousand years ago in the Roman Empire the December festival was called Saturnalia. People decorated their houses with evergreen plants, they exchanged gifts and wore fancy hats at their fairs and parties.

In Scandinavia the Norse people held their own winter celebration. This was called the Yule Festival. They burned great logs in honour of the gods Odin and Thor and drank a strong alcoholic drink called mead. Mistletoe was used as a decoration.

"When Christianity began to spread across Europe," continued Mrs Thomas, "there was already a long history of celebration and merry-making in December. After all, the shortest day in December is something to celebrate. It means the darkness of winter is at its worst and that the hours of daylight will increase. No one actually knows on what day Jesus was born. It probably seemed natural to the early Christians to celebrate the new life of Jesus at the time when Europeans had always celebrated the New Year and the hope it brings for the future.

100

The mayor switches on the Christmas lights in Exeter city centre. Light and fire were the symbols of many ancient winter festivals.

Guides from a church company bring toys for the National Children's Home to a special service before Christmas.

102

"The old celebrations were given a Christian meaning but of course many of the practices have continued right down to the present day. Take this holly, for example. It has been used as decoration for centuries. It is a symbol of eternal life because, unlike most plants, in winter it keeps its colour."

Nina had been waiting for Mrs Thomas to mention the most obvious feature of Christmas. "What about Father Christmas? How long have people believed in him?"

Mrs Thomas replied that the name Father Christmas was quite a recent one. "The idea of Father Christmas came to Britain from the U.S.A. about a hundred and fifty years ago. We must go back much further to find out about the model for Father Christmas, the character we call Santa Claus.

"More than sixteen hundred years ago there was a bishop called Nicholas who lived in Asia Minor. He spent part of his life in prison, during a period of persecution by the Emperor Diocletian. Hardly anything is known about Nicholas except that he died on 6 December in A.D. 326. His remains were taken to Bari in Italy in A.D. 1087 and they are still there.

"Many legends developed about Bishop Nicholas, or Saint Nicholas as he was now known. You may have heard the stories about how he left money on poor people's doorsteps. He is certainly believed to have been very kind to children, and to have given them many presents.

"Sailors used to take a statue of St Nicholas with them on their voyages. They believed he would bring them good fortune. Dutch sailors called him 'Sinter Klaus', and that is how we got the name Santa Claus. In Norway Santa Claus was said to ride over rooftops on a sleigh pulled by reindeer from Lapland. Add all those traditions together and you have a story about an old man riding a sleigh over rooftops and leaving presents for children.

"We Christians exchange gifts at Christmas because we remember how, in the Bible story, wise men brought gifts to Jesus. When we give or receive a gift we also remember God's gift of Jesus to the earth."

Nina joined in the Christmas celebrations until late that

night. The family enjoyed a traditional Christmas dinner and afterwards they played party games and danced to the records Susan and Nina had brought along. Grandad dozed off in the chair, full of Christmas cheer. Gary had to remove his pipe very carefully from his mouth.

The following day the whole meal was staged again. This time Grandma and Grandad went to Susan and Gary's. The Thomas family always celebrate Christmas Day at Grandma's and Boxing Day at their own home.

Nina asked Grandad why the day was called Boxing Day.

"Two reasons, Nina. In the past, before we had anything like pensions or social security benefits, each church kept a box called a poor-box, where the congregation could put in a donation every week. All the boxes were emptied on 26 December and the money was given to the poor of the parish.

"The second reason is the old custom of servants and apprentices saving gifts and tips in a box of their own. Most tips were given at Christmas so the boxes were opened the day after Christmas – hence the name Boxing Day."

"So there is nothing religious about Boxing Day?" asked Nina.

"Oh, yes," replied Grandad. "Boxing Day has a Christian title too. We call it St Stephen's Day. Stephen was the first Christian to be killed for his beliefs. We call such a person a **martyr**. He was later made a saint and given a special place in the Christian calendar, the day after Jesus's birthday."

Gary was busy counting his money. He was adding the money he had received from relatives to his tips from the paper round.

"Now that Christmas is almost over, I'll be able to spend all this. The sales start tomorrow."

Nina seemed surprised. "I can't get used to how short your Christian festivals are. We Hindus have our Navaratri and Dasshera festivals in autumn that go on for ten days. During that time we meet each night to sing, dance and pray. At the end of the tenth day we are exhausted. Most nights we don't get home till midnight."

Christmas crib, with figures of the shepherds and the wise men, made by pupils of an Anglican Church school

Mrs Thomas interrupted to say Gary was quite wrong to believe that Christians ended after Boxing Day. "Christmas isn't over until 6 January, at **Epiphany**. This word means 'appearance' and it is then that Christians believe the wise men visited Jesus. The three gifts they carried have a special meaning for us Christians."

"Do you mean gold, frankincense and myrrh, Mum?" asked Gary.

"That's right. Gold represents royalty, frankincense divinity and myrrh death. To us they are symbols of Jesus, the divine King who died and rose again to give the rest of us the chance of a new life in God. In this family, Nina, we keep the old traditions. The Christmas decorations will stay up until Epiphany, which we call Twelfth Night. Only then will they be taken down."

15
Christianity in Britain

Christianity has had an enormous influence on Britain over the last fifteen hundred years. The evidence is all around us. When we fill in forms we sometimes find they ask for our "Christian name". Long ago virtually everyone in Britain was a Christian and all records were kept by the churches so names were truly Christian names. Nowadays Britain has a much more varied population. The word "forename" has replaced "Christian name" on many official forms, but not all. There have been Jews in Britain for hundreds of years but more recently large numbers of people of other faiths have settled here: Hindus from India and East Africa, Muslims from Pakistan, Bangladesh, India, East Africa, Nigeria and the Middle East, Sikhs from India and East Africa, Jews from Europe, Buddhists from Sri Lanka and Vietnam, as well as Chinese people who have their own religious traditions. Just as there are Christian churches in Pakistan, India, China, Africa and the Middle East, so there are now mosques, temples and gurdwaras in Britain.

The names of the streets, areas and towns in which we live, even the railway stations we use, may have a Christian origin. St Bartholomew's Hospital, St Pancras' Station, St Helens town all derive their names from our Christian past.

Most countries with large Christian populations have a patron saint, a Christian saint whom they adopt as their special saint. In Britain we have four patron saints: Andrew for Scotland, David for Wales, George for England and Patrick for Ireland. All that is known about St George is that he was killed for his beliefs in Palestine about seventeen hundred years ago. Since then legends have developed about

Epstein's statue of St Michael and the Devil at Coventry Cathedral

Stained-glass window representing St George killing the dragon, a legend that dates from the twelfth century

him. The English celebrate his day, 23 April, as their special national day and his flag, a red cross on a white background, has been used in England for over six hundred years.

The dating system we use was created by Pope Gregory XIII in 1582. Until then Europeans had used a system of dating originally established by Julius Caesar. Unfortunately it was inaccurate. The new calendar that replaced it was named after Pope Gregory and is known as the Gregorian Calendar. This divides up the whole of history. The division point is the birth of Jesus. Anything that happened before then is dated B.C. (Before Christ); everything since is dated A.D. (Anno Domini – translated from the Latin this means "in the year of our Lord").

Many aspects of all our lives are influenced by our Christian heritage. The official State religion of part of Britain remains the Christianity of the Church of England. The Prime Minister is involved in choosing Anglican bishops. Many of the laws in Britain have Christian origins. They apply to all the people whether or not they are Christians. For example, in Britain it is against the law for men and women to have more than one wife or husband at a time. It is also possible to be jailed for saying something offensive about God.

The superstitions that people hold often have their origins in Christian belief. Number thirteen is considered unlucky. On some streets there is no number thirteen. Floor number twelve of a multi-storey building may be followed by number fourteen. This superstition recalls the Last Supper, when thirteen people sat around the table before the betrayal of Jesus. Friday the thirteenth is regarded as a day when bad luck is likely to occur. The combination of Friday, the day on which Jesus died, with thirteen, the number of people at the Last Supper, gave rise to this widely held belief.

Walking under a ladder is believed to be unlucky. In the past the triangle represented belief in the Trinity of God the Father, God the Son and God the Holy Ghost. To walk under a ladder was to break the Trinity.

Many challenges face Christians today. One of the greatest is how the Christian community should respond to the changes taking place in Britain and how it should relate to the growing number of non-Christians in the country. Apart from practising Christians Britain is now home for Jews, Muslims, Sikhs, Hindus, Buddhists, Jains, agnostics, who are not sure whether or not there is a God, and atheists, who believe there is no such thing as God.

In many parts of the world the Churches are the only defenders of the poor and the persecuted. In certain countries bishops and priests speak out against the action of cruel governments, sometimes risking their lives in the process. In various countries of Central and South America, where some governments do little to help the poor, the bishops, priests and nuns provide a voice for the people. They sometimes support the poor in fighting for a better life and then find themselves under attack from the Government.

In the 1980s bishops in Britain began to call on the Government to slow down the rate of unemployment and help those out of work. This caused a great fuss because many people in Britain don't think bishops should become involved in such matters.

The Churches in Britain are asking themselves what role they should play. Should they contribute to debates about unemployment, foreign affairs, nuclear disarmament and poverty? Some Christians believe the Church should leave such matters to politicians. Others see the issues as central to our lives and therefore of great concern to all Christians.

The Christian Churches in Britain must decide their own future. Will they draw together as a broader Christian community or maintain their separate identities? Will the ordination of women as priests in some Churches around the world lead to women priests being accepted in the larger British denominations?

To many Christians this is an exciting and stimulating period in Church history. They know they are involved in helping to choose the way their religion will develop. There

Bishop Butler at a Vigil for Disarmament outside Westminster Abbey

are sure to be disagreements, but, where religion is concerned, that isn't unusual.

Christians have their own way of seeing the world. They have a view of the kind of world they hope to see develop and most believe that they have a great deal to offer our society. To learn more about how Christians view the world and how they think of their God you need to talk to Christians themselves. In this book we have scratched the surface of Christianity. There is much more to discover if you care to dig deeper.

SUGGESTIONS FOR FURTHER STUDY

1 There was a period in history when Christmas celebrations were forbidden in Britain by an Act of Parliament. When and why did this happen?

2 Forenames often have meanings; for example, Peter means "rock". Find out what your own forename means.

3 Christians often disagree about how they should respond to the world's problems. How would you expect a Christian to feel about
(a) capital punishment
(b) unemployment
(c) nuclear weapons?

4 The days of the week and months of the year have their origins outside Christianity. Try to discover how each got its name.

5 Write a paragraph about each of the following:
(a) St Patrick
(b) St George
(c) St Andrew
(d) St David
Include a sketch of the special symbol associated with each saint.

Resources/Useful Addresses

It is neither possible nor practical to list all the books and other resource material available on Christianity; the following suggestions are only a small selection. Most of the publishers and other organizations mentioned will of course supply copies of their own catalogues, and a few useful addresses are included at the end of this section. Further details of many of the items can also be found in *World Religions: A Handbook for Teachers*, edited by W. Owen Cole and published by the Commission for Racial Equality.

BOOKS FOR PUPILS
Bible Stories for Today: The Old Testament; The New Testament. J. G. Priestley. R.M.E.P.
Christian Worship; Christian Celebrations; Christian Objects. C.E.M.
Christian Worship; Exploring the Bible; Jesus. Chichester Project, Lutterworth.
Christmas; Easter; Holy Week; Shrove Tuesday, Ash Wednesday and Mardi Gras, and others. Living Festivals Series, R.M.E.P.
The Church of England; The Roman Catholic Church; The United Reformed Church, and others. Christian Denominations Series, R.M.E.P.
Churches and Cathedrals. Ladybird.
Churches in Britain, I. Calvert. Blackwell.
A Day with a Vicar, Chris Fairclough. Wayland.
Good News Bible (colour illustrated edition). Collins/ Fontana.
The Lion Encyclopedia of the Bible. Lion.
Religious Buildings and Festivals, J. R. Bailey. Schofield & Sims.

Visiting an Anglican Church; Visiting a Roman Catholic Church, and others. Lutterworth.
What to look for inside a Church; What to look for outside a Church. Ladybird.

BOOKS FOR TEACHERS

A Bedside Book for R.E. Teachers, T. Copley and D. Easton. S.C.M.
The Church in the World. C.E.M.
Festivals, R. Manning-Saunders. Heinemann.
Living Together: A Teachers' Handbook of Suggestions for Religious Education. City of Birmingham District Council Education Committee.
Religion in the Multi-Faith School: A Tool for Teachers, W. Owen Cole (ed.). Hulton.
Religious Education in Secondary Schools; Religious Education in Primary Schools. Schools Council Working Papers 36 and 44, Evans/Methuen Educational.
Six Religions in the Twentieth Century, W. Owen Cole (ed.). Hulton.
Teaching Religion in School: A Practical Approach, J. Holm. O.U.P.
The Trial of Jesus of Nazareth, S. C. F. Brandon. Manchester University Press.
What Can I Do in R.E.?, M. Grimmitt. Mayhew-McCrimmon.

SLIDES AND FILMSTRIPS

The Founder of Christianity; The Growth of Christianity; The English Parish Church; The Life of Christ Seen Through the Eyes of the Artist, and other filmstrips. VP Audio-visual Resources.
People at Worship slidefolios series (includes *Christian Churches: The Significant Features; Christian Symbols; Christian Worship; Christian Initiation; A Christian Wedding); Water in the Third World.* Rickitt Educational Media.

114

PICTURES AND POSTERS
Christianity (set of photographs); *Easter Posters* (Primary) and *Easter Posters* (Secondary); *Christianity in View* (posters). C.E.M.
Discovering Religion in Life and Action (photopack). Lutterworth.
Palestine in the Life of Christ; Initiation Rites/Birth Rites/Marriage Rites/Death Rites; Christian Festivals; World Water Decade (all posters). Also *Water* (photopack). Pictorial Charts Educational Trust.

WORKSHEETS
Christianity (Topic Folder No. 1); *Discovering the Church.* C.E.M.

FILMS/VIDEO
Christianity through the Eyes of Christian Children. C.E.M. Video.
Christmas Down and Out (black-and-white film); *Sweetwater Safari* (UNICEF colour film). Concord Films Council.

USEFUL ADDRESSES
C.E.M. (Christian Education Movement), 2 Chester House, Pages Lane, London N10 1PR.
C.I.O. (Church Information Office), Church House, Dean's Yard, Westminster, London SW1P 3NZ.
Commission for Racial Equality, Elliot House, 10–12 Allington Street, London SW1E 5EH.
Concord Films Council Ltd, 201 Felixstowe Road, Ipswich, Suffolk IP3 9BJ.
Pictorial Charts Educational Trust, 27 Kirchen Road, London W13 0UD.
Rickitt Educational Media, Ilton, Ilminster, Somerset TA19 9HS.
VP Audio-visual Resources, The Green, Northleach, Cheltenham, Gloucestershire GL54 3EX.

Glossary

Advent	literally, "coming". The season before Christmas, beginning on the fourth Sunday before the festival. It marks the beginning of the Christian year.
aisle	passage between the pews in a church.
alms	money given to help others.
altar	Communion table.
Anglican	member of the Anglican Church (or Anglican Communion), the Church of England.
Apostle	title given to the first disciples chosen by Jesus, and also to St Paul.
archbishop	chief bishop.
Ascension Day	the sixth Thursday (the fortieth day) after Easter, when Jesus is believed to have ascended into heaven.
Ash Wednesday	the first day of Lent.
Baptist	member of a Protestant Christian denomination which initiates candidates by total immersion, rather than by infant baptism.
baptize	to initiate into a religious faith by a baptism ceremony.
Bible	the holy book of Christianity, comprising the Old Testament and the New Testament, or the Hebrew Bible, the holy book of the Jews, comprising only the Old Testament.
bishop	clergyman who supervises a diocese.

116

candidate	literally, "robed in white". Person seeking membership of a Church.
cassock	long, loose robe worn especially by clergymen and members of the choir.
cathedral	principal church in a diocese.
chalice	cup used to hold the wine during the celebration of the Eucharist.
chancel	part of a Christian church near the altar, to the east of the nave, used especially by the clergy.
chapel	Nonconformist church; building used for private worship.
Christianity	religion of the followers of Jesus Christ (Christians).
Christmas	Christian festival celebrating the birth of Jesus.
Christmas carol	joyful hymn sung at Christmas time.
church	building for Christian worship; Church, the community of all Christians throughout the world, or a Christian denomination.
Church of England	the Anglican Communion.
clergyman	ordained minister approved to lead religious worship.
confirmation	ceremony performed in some Churches for those wishing to make a deeper Christian commitment, to become full members of their Church.
congregation	group of people gathered together, usually in a church or chapel, for religious worship.
Creed	formal statement of faith used in the Western Christian Church. The Apostles' Creed and the Nicene Creed are two versions of the Creed.
crematorium	place where corpses are burnt.

117

Crucifixion	the death of Jesus on the cross.
denomination	Church or religious sect following particular religious beliefs.
diocese	district governed by a bishop and divided into parishes, each in the care of a priest.
disciple	an early believer in Jesus, especially the first twelve followers of Jesus, the Apostles, and the seventy followers mentioned in Luke 10:1–16.
Easter	the most joyful Christian festival, commemorating Jesus's resurrection on Easter Day (Easter Sunday).
ecumenical	representing all Christians, whatever their denomination.
Epiphany	literally, "manifestation" or "appearance". The day when the Magi or wise men from the East (by tradition, three kings) came to see the infant Jesus.
Eucharist	literally, "thanksgiving". Christian ceremony of Holy Communion in which bread and wine are consumed in memory of Jesus. The bread is a reminder of Jesus's body, the wine of his blood.
font	receptacle for holy water used in Christian baptism.
Good Friday	the Friday before Easter Day. It commemorates the Crucifixion.
gospel	literally, "good news". The message of hope brought by Jesus. The four Gospels of Matthew, Mark, Luke and John in the New Testament record Jesus's life and teachings.
hearse	vehicle used to transport coffins.
Holy Communion	taking part in the Eucharist.

Holy Spirit or Holy Ghost. The third person of the Christian Holy Trinity. The "comforter" or "counsellor" Jesus promised to his disciples before he ascended into heaven, often regarded by Christians as the means by which God acts on earth.

Holy Trinity the three persons or parts of the Christian God: Father, Son and Holy Spirit.

Holy Week the week before Easter Day.

Last Supper the last meal Jesus took with his disciples before his arrest. The Eucharist is based on this meal.

lectern desk from which the lessons (readings from the Bible, etc.) are read during church services.

Lent the period of forty days (not including Sundays) of penitence beginning on Ash Wednesday and ending on Holy Saturday, the day before Easter Day.

martyr person killed for his/her beliefs.

Maundy Thursday literally, "Commandment" Thursday. The Thursday of Holy Week, the day of the Last Supper, when Jesus instituted the Eucharist.

Messiah Hebrew name for the promised deliverer of the Jews; a name given to Jesus by Christians.

minister man or woman approved to lead religious worship. Title favoured by many Nonconformist Churches.

miracle play (or mystery play) drama based on the life of Jesus or the saints, medieval in origin.

missionary person sent, often abroad, by a

119

	religious body to tell others of his/her religious faith.
monk	member of a religious community of men living under the vows of poverty, chastity and obedience.
myth	traditional story intended to convey ideas rather than historical facts.
nave	part of a Christian church from the west wall to the chancel, used especially by the congregation.
New Testament	the twenty-seven books that form the second part of the Christian Bible. They include the four Gospels, the Acts of the Apostles and the Epistles of St Paul.
Nonconformist Churches	Christian Churches in Britain other than the Roman Catholic Church or the Church of England.
nun	member of a women's religious order living under the vows of poverty, chastity and obedience.
Old Testament	the thirty-nine books that form the first part of the Christian Bible, corresponding to the scriptures in the Hebrew Bible of the Jewish religion.
ordain	admit as a minister of the Christian Church. In the Orthodox, Anglican and Roman Catholic Churches bishops confer ordination. In the Nonconformist Churches, which recognize only one order of ministers, ordination is carried out by senior ministers.
Palm Sunday	the Sunday before Easter Day; the last Sunday in Lent.
parable	allegory, or story, used to clarify a religious or moral teaching.

120

parish	area with its own church and in the care of an Anglican vicar or Roman Catholic priest.
paten	shallow plate on which the bread is placed during the celebration of the Eucharist.
Pentecost	Jewish festival of Shavuot, commemorating the giving of the Ten Commandments to Moses; the Christian festival of Pentecost is more commonly known as Whitsun.
Pentecostal Church	Protestant denomination that stresses the activity of the Holy Spirit.
pew	seat in a church, usually a fixed bench with a back, sometimes enclosed.
pope	the Bishop of Rome, originally the leader of the Christian Church in Western Europe; now, the leader of the Roman Catholic Church.
priest	Roman Catholic or Anglican minister.
Protestant	member of a Western Christian Church other than the Roman Catholic Church.
pulpit	raised platform in a church, usually with a desk, from which sermons are delivered.
rabbi	Jewish religious teacher and leader.
resurrection	coming to life again.
Roman Catholic	member of the Church that acknowledges the pope as its head.
rood	crucifix, especially one on a rood-screen.
rood-screen	stone or wooden screen dividing the nave and chancel in a church.
sermon	religious speech.
Shrove Tuesday	the day before Ash Wednesday,

when Christians traditionally were "shriven", confessing their sins and being forgiven. Also called Pancake Day or Mardi Gras.

stole   long strip of cloth worn around the neck by the clergy.

synagogue   place of Jewish religious worship.

temple   place of Hindu, Buddhist, etc. religious worship; Temple, any of the three Temples built in Jerusalem by the Jews for religious worship.

Twelve Disciples   *see* disciples.

vestments   official garments worn by the clergy or members of the choir during religious services.

vestry   room in a church where vestments are kept and put on.

vicar   Church of England clergyman, usually in charge of a parish or a group of parishes.

Whitsun   Whit Sunday (originally, "White Sunday"). The Christian festival of Pentecost, commemorating the gift of the Holy Spirit.